First, rinse the corn in cold water and make sure there are no rocks or pieces of cob mixed in. Then put the corn in a pot and add cold water so that the corn is well covered. Next, prepare the lime. For 1 kilo (2.2 pounds) of corn, put 1 heaping tablespoon of lime in a bowl and add 1 cup of cold water. If the lime is fresh, it will begin to sizzle and give off heat from the chemical reaction. This process is known as slaking. If the lime is older, it will take longer to slake. Stir it once, then let it sit. Some residue will settle to the bottom. After the lime has slaked, bring the corn to a low simmer and add half of the lime water. The corn will turn a vibrant yellow right away. Then taste a couple of drops of the liquid on your tongue. You should detect a slightly acrid, burning sensation. If not, add more lime solution and taste again. If it's too strong, add some water and taste again. Cook the corn until the skins separate easily from the kernels, which takes about 20 minutes. Let the corn sit in the water overnight.

The next day, drain the corn, rinse it, and drain again. After that, grind it in a hand-mill such as a Corona or, like the Mexicans of old (and probably still a few today), with a *mano* and *metate*, made from porous volcanic stone. The mano is the rolling pin-like piece and the metate is the rectangular, slightly curved stone with short legs. Once ground, the resulting masa, or dough, can be patted or pressed into tortillas, or dried for future use. Obviously, I have not advanced the art of tortilla making here, but only given a glimpse. I believe it's a lot like chess: a day to learn, a lifetime to master.

SALSAS AND SIDES

Tomato-Based Salsas
Fresh Tomato Salsa
Sierra-Style Tomato Salsa
Quick Tomato Salsa

Chile-Based Salsas
Poblano and Jalapeño Salsa
Chile de Árbol Salsa
Don Felix Red Salsa
Seven Chile Salsa

Green and Avocado Salsas
Fresh Tomatillo Salsa
La Esquina Taquería's Green Salsa
Tomatillo and Chile de Árbol Salsa
Chunky Guacamole
Avocado and Jalapeño Salsa

Sides
Baja Coleslaw with Shrimp
Whole Pinto Beans
Rice with Vegetables
Roasted Poblano Chile Strips
Pickled Jalapeños and Carrots
Pickled Chipotles

FRESH TOMATO SALSA
Salsa Fresca de Tomate

Nothing satisfies like a fresh tomato salsa in the middle of summer. Scooped up on corn chips or piled liberally on the tacos of the day, the mélange of ingredients creates an irresistible symphony of fresh flavor. With red tomatoes, green cilantro, and red onions, it is as pleasing to look at as it is to taste. Triple or quadruple this recipe at the height of the season because there's never enough.

Note: *When serving on tacos, use a slotted spoon to drain excess liquid. Watery tacos aren't much fun! If possible use paste tomatoes because they have less free water content.*

MAKES ABOUT 2 CUPS

> 1 pound tomatoes
> 2 tablespoons finely chopped red onion
> 2 tablespoons chopped cilantro
> 1 jalapeño or serrano chile, stemmed and minced (seed and devein for a milder salsa)
> Juice of 1 lime (approximately 2 tablespoons)
> Zest of 1 lime (optional)
> Salt

1. Dice the tomatoes and put them in a strainer or colander to drain some of their water, about 2 minutes. Transfer them to a medium-size bowl.

2. Add the onion, cilantro, jalapeño, lime juice, and lime zest, if using, and salt to taste. Mix well. Cover and refrigerate until ready to use. The salsa will keep in the refrigerator for a week or longer, though the onion flavor will grow stronger.

SIERRA-STYLE TOMATO SALSA
Salsa Roja de la Sierra

I love anything that has been cooked over a coal or wood fire. Somehow, even food that has been charred in a pan on the stove has a satisfying campfire-like quality. The authentic texture of this salsa comes from the ingredients being mashed in a *molcajete*. These stone mortars are widely available in Mexican markets, and in addition to creating a salsa with excellent texture, they double as a stylish serving dish. The *cebolletas* found in Mexican markets are similar to scallions, but the white base is a little bulb. Use scallions if cebolletas are unavailable. I use serrano chiles in the recipe because they have a fruitiness beneath the heat.

Note: *For a slightly more refined salsa, peel and seed the serranos and tomatoes before adding.*

MAKES ABOUT 2 CUPS

>   1 cebolleta or scallion
>   1 teaspoon olive oil
>   2 small cloves garlic, peeled
>   3 serrano chiles
>   3 medium tomatoes
>   1 teaspoon salt

1. Preheat a *comal*, or a medium-size cast-iron pan, over medium-high heat for 5 minutes.

2. In a small bowl, lightly coat the cebolleta with the olive oil to prevent drying while cooking.

3. On the comal, cook the cebolleta and garlic, turning them frequently until they brown lightly. Set aside and let cool. Cook the serranos and tomatoes until they brown and their skins blister. Set aside and let cool.

4. In a stone mortar, or food processor or blender, mash or pulse the cebolleta, garlic, and salt until incorporated. Stem and roughly chop the serranos, then mash or pulse them with the cebolleta mixture.

5. Core and roughly chop the tomatoes, reserving the liquid. Add the tomatoes and liquid to the cebolleta mixture, and mash or pulse to incorporate.

6. Pour the salsa into a bowl or container. Cover and refrigerate until ready to use. The salsa will keep in the refrigerator for a week or longer, though the onion and garlic flavors will grow stronger.

QUICK TOMATO SALSA
Salsa Rápida de los Guys

This simple and quick salsa always comes through in a pinch. I learned it from *los guys*, my fellow cooks in the kitchen of Gordon Biersch Brewery in Palo Alto, where I worked at the time. For the morning snack, I would usually warm a few dozen corn tortillas and make a big pan of scrambled eggs spiked with onions and garlic. One of the prep cooks would throw the salsa ingredients into a pot of water and cook it up in time to serve with the tacos. It's surprisingly delicious for being so uncomplicated.

MAKES ABOUT 2 CUPS

> 4 medium tomatoes
> 1 small white onion, peeled
> 2 or 3 jalapeño chiles, stemmed
> Salt

1. In a medium-size pot, combine the tomatoes, onion, and jalapeños, and cover them with water. Bring to a boil, then simmer for 5 minutes.

2. With a slotted spoon, remove the ingredients from the pot and put them in a food processor or blender. Blend until smooth, about 1 minute. Add salt to taste.

3. Pour the salsa into a bowl or container. Cover and refrigerate until ready to use. The salsa will keep in the refrigerator for a week or longer, though the onion flavor will grow stronger.

POBLANO AND JALAPEÑO SALSA
Salsa de Chiles Poblano y Jalapeño

I first tasted this little gem of a condiment at the fish taco stall Tacos La Tía in Ensenada. Fire-roasting the chiles creates an incomparable flavor, elevating their essence while adding a rustic, rancho-style touch. This salsa, blended with Mexican Crema (see page 10), is also *fantástico* on grilled flap steak and grilled chicken.

MAKES 1¼ CUPS

> 4 fresh poblano chiles
> 1 jalapeño chile
> Olive oil (if roasting on an electric range)

1. Light a burner on the stove and set the poblanos directly on the burner grate, one or two at a time, turning occasionally, until the entire chile is blackened. (If you have an electric stove, heat a cast-iron pan over medium-high heat. In a small bowl, coat the poblanos lightly with oil and blacken them in the pan.)

2. Put the poblanos in a bowl, covered, until cool. Peel the blackened skins off the poblanos. Cut the poblanos open and remove the stem and all of the seeds. Do not rinse the poblanos in water at any time. Put the poblano pieces in a food processor or blender.

3. Cut the jalapeño in half lengthwise. Remove the stem and seeds. Chop the jalapeño into chunks and add half of it to the poblanos. Purée until smooth. Add the other half if you desire more heat.

4. Pour the salsa into a bowl or container. Cover and refrigerate until ready to use. The salsa will keep in the refrigerator for two weeks or longer.

CHILE DE ÁRBOL SALSA
Salsa de Chile de Árbol

The *chile de árbol* is a workhorse, used throughout Mexico to make fiery table salsas. The earthy, slightly grassy flavor of these slender, deep red pods combines well with garlic and a touch of salt. The ensuing blend, a welcome but not overwhelming splash of fire, is a must in the arsenal of the serious taco-head. They are widely available in Latin American markets and the ethnic sections of supermarkets.

MAKES ABOUT 2 CUPS

> 2 ounces dried chiles de árbol (60 to 70 pods)
> 2 cloves garlic, roughly chopped
> Salt

1. In a small pot, bring about 2 cups of water to a boil.

2. Meanwhile, stem the chiles. Using two bowls, break each chile in half and roll the pieces between your fingers over one bowl to catch the seeds. Put the chile pieces in the other bowl, discarding the bowl of seeds. (It isn't necessary to remove every seed; leaving a small percentage won't affect the salsa.)

3. Pour the hot water over the chiles until they are just covered. Cover the bowl with a plate or lid. Let it sit for 30 minutes, stirring once or twice.

4. With a slotted spoon, remove the chiles and put them in a food processor or blender. Pour some soaking water over the chiles until it comes halfway up the chiles. Add the garlic and salt to taste. Blend the mixture until it is a smooth purée. The consistency should be slightly thick yet pourable. Add more water, a little at a time, if necessary.

5. Pour the salsa into a bowl or container. Cover and refrigerate until ready to use. The salsa will keep in the refrigerator for a week or longer, though the garlic flavor will grow stronger.

DON FELIX RED SALSA
Salsa Roja Don Felix

While on a West L.A. taco tour, I got on famously with the cook at Carnicería Don Felix. She even let me hang out in the kitchen. In addition to *cuerito* (pigskin sautéed in lard) and *barbacoa* (steamed beef) tacos, I had a *cabeza* (beef head) taco topped with a smacking-hot red salsa. The señora obliged me when I asked what was in her salsa. Here I present my version.

MAKES ABOUT 2 CUPS

> 2 ounces dried *chiles de árbol* (60 to 70 pods)
> ½ white onion, roughly chopped
> 2 cloves garlic
> ½ teaspoon cumin seed
> Salt
> 1 tablespoon finely chopped cilantro

1. In a small pot, bring about 2 cups of water to a boil.

2. Meanwhile, stem the chiles. Using two bowls, break each chile in half and roll the pieces between your fingers over one bowl to catch the seeds. Put the chile pieces in the other bowl, discarding the bowl of seeds. (It isn't necessary to remove every seed; leaving a small percentage won't affect the salsa.)

3. Pour the hot water over the chiles until they are just covered. Cover the bowl with a plate or lid. Let it sit for 30 minutes, stirring once or twice.

4. With a slotted spoon, remove the chiles and put them in a food processor or blender. Pour some soaking water over the chiles until it comes halfway up the chiles. Add the onion, garlic, cumin, and salt to taste. Blend the mixture until it is a smooth purée. The consistency should be slightly thick yet pourable. Add more water, little by little, if necessary.

5. Pour the salsa into a bowl or container and stir in the cilantro. Cover and refrigerate until ready to use. The salsa will keep in the refrigerator for a week or longer, though the onion and garlic flavors will grow stronger.

SEVEN CHILE SALSA
Salsa de Siete Chiles

This salsa is so many things at once: rich, tangy, smoky, and sweet. It's even good on vanilla ice cream. Make this salsa a day or two in advance to allow the flavors to marry completely.

MAKES 2¼ CUPS

> 1 *pasilla* chile
> 1 ancho chile
> 1 *morita* chile
> 2 dried chipotle chiles
> 2 *cascabel* chiles
> 2 *guajillo* chiles
> 2 *chiles de árbol*
> ½ cup vegetable oil
> 1 large tomato, finely chopped
> 6 cloves garlic, roughly chopped
> 1 teaspoon finely chopped epazote (optional)
> 1 teaspoon finely chopped cilantro
> ½ cup cider vinegar
> ½ teaspoon salt
> ¾ cup agave nectar

1. On a *comal*, or in a medium-size cast-iron pan, over medium heat, lightly toast the pasilla, ancho, morita, chipotles, cascabels, guajillos, and chiles de árbol. Set them aside to cool, then stem, seed, and break them into pieces.

2. In a medium-size sauté pan over medium heat, heat the oil. Then add the chiles, tomato, and garlic. Cook about 5 minutes, stirring occasionally. Add the epazote, if using, and the cilantro and cook 5 minutes longer. Reduce the heat to low and cook 3 minutes longer. Set pan aside to cool.

3. Pour the chile mixture from the pan into a food processor or blender. Add the vinegar and salt and blend until smooth. Pour the salsa into a medium-size bowl and stir in the agave nectar until well incorporated. Cover and refrigerate until ready to use. The salsa will keep in the refrigerator for two weeks or longer.

FRESH TOMATILLO SALSA
Salsa Fresca de Tomatillo

If you can get them, use purple tomatillos in this recipe. Since they're not cooked, they stay purple, a nice visual touch to an already tasty salsa.

MAKES ABOUT 2 CUPS

 1 pound tomatillos, husks removed
 2 tablespoons finely chopped red onion
 2 tablespoons chopped cilantro
 1 jalapeño or serrano chile, stemmed and minced (seed and devein for a
   milder salsa)
 Juice of 1 lime (approximately 2 tablespoons)
 Zest of 1 lime (optional)
 Salt

Dice the tomatillos and put them in a medium-size bowl. Add the onion, cilantro, jalapeño, lime juice, and lime zest, if using, and salt to taste. Mix well. Cover and refrigerate until ready to use. The salsa will keep in the refrigerator for a week or longer, though the onion flavor will grow stronger.

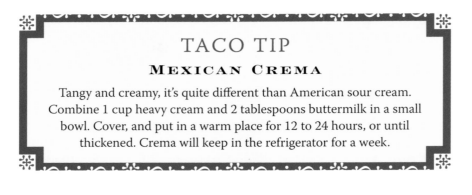

TACO TIP
MEXICAN CREMA
Tangy and creamy, it's quite different than American sour cream. Combine 1 cup heavy cream and 2 tablespoons buttermilk in a small bowl. Cover, and put in a warm place for 12 to 24 hours, or until thickened. Crema will keep in the refrigerator for a week.

LA ESQUINA TAQUERÍA'S GREEN SALSA

Salsa Verde de La Esquina Taquería

This creamy and tangy salsa from chef Jose Alvarado of La Esquina in New York City accompanies his Pork Loin in Chile Adobo with Grilled Pineapple (see page 55).

MAKES ABOUT 2 CUPS

 5 tomatillos, husks removed, quartered
 ½ medium white onion, roughly chopped
 2 jalapeño chiles, stemmed and roughly chopped
 2 cloves garlic, roughly chopped
 1 large avocado, peeled, pitted, and roughly chopped
 2 tablespoons cilantro
 1 teaspoon sugar
 Juice of 1 lime (approximately 2 tablespoons)
 ¼ cup water
 Salt

1. Place the tomatillos, onion, jalapeños, garlic, avocado, cilantro, sugar, lime juice, water, and salt to taste in a food processor or blender and blend until smooth.

2. Pour the salsa into a bowl or container. Cover and refrigerate until ready to use. The salsa will keep in the refrigerator for 1 to 2 days.

TOMATILLO AND CHILE DE ÁRBOL SALSA
Salsa de Tomatillo y Chile de Árbol

The tangy flavor of the tomatillos blends very nicely with the earthy piquancy of the *chile de árbol*. It tones down the heat and makes a salsa that is nearly drinkable. Roasting the tomatillos on the grill or on a griddle adds flavor and nice little blackened specks to the salsa. Inspiration for this salsa comes from Tacomiendo in Culver City, California.

MAKES ABOUT 3 CUPS

    1 pound tomatillos, husks removed
    1 cup Chile de Árbol Salsa (see page 6)
    Salt

1. Put the tomatillos in a pot with just enough water to cover them. Bring the water almost to a boil, then turn the heat down to low. Cook the tomatillos until soft, about 10 minutes. Don't overcook or they will split. (Alternately, you can roast them on a *comal*, in a medium-size cast-iron pan on the stove, or on a charcoal grill, until browned and softened, about 10 minutes.)

2. With a slotted spoon, transfer the tomatillos to a food processor or blender, reserving the cooking water. Purée until smooth, or just pulse a few times if you prefer a chunkier salsa. Add a little of the reserved cooking water to the tomatillos if you wish to thin the salsa.

3. In a medium-size bowl, combine the tomatillos and the Chile de Árbol Salsa. Add salt to taste. Cover and refrigerate until ready to use. The salsa will keep in the refrigerator for a week or longer, though the garlic flavor will grow stronger.

CHUNKY GUACAMOLE
Guacamole Casero

The velvety richness of avocados (high-oil types such as Haas), flecked with bits of sun-ripened tomato, cilantro, and piquant white onion, guarantees this "guac" will be a hit.

MAKES 1½ CUPS

> 2 large avocados, peeled and pitted
> 2 tablespoons finely chopped white onion
> 2 tablespoons finely chopped cilantro
> 1 medium tomato, finely chopped
> Salt

1. Put the avocados in a *molcajete* (a traditional stone mortar), or a medium-size bowl, crushing them with the *mano* (a pestle), or a fork, until they are a chunky paste. Add the onion, cilantro, and tomato. Stir. Add salt to taste.

2. Cover tightly with plastic wrap and refrigerate until ready to serve. If the surface of the guacamole begins to darken, stir thoroughly before serving. The salsa will keep in the refrigerator for 1 day.

AVOCADO AND JALAPEÑO SALSA
Salsa de Aguacate y Jalapeño

I'm traveling down the California coast on a cold winter night. In Atascadero there's a little kiosk that has a real *trompo*, or vertical spit, cooking pork *al pastor* tacos exclusively. This avocado salsa catches my fancy. It's both creamy and spicy, the jalapeño and raw onion asserting themselves in perfect balance with the rich avocado. Prepare it no more than an hour or two before serving, just enough time for the flavors to marry without allowing the avocado to darken.

Variation: *For a very hot salsa, substitute a habanero for the jalapeño.*

MAKES 1½ CUPS

> 3 avocados, peeled and pitted
> 1 jalapeño chile, stemmed and seeded
> 2 tablespoons minced white onion, divided
> Salt

1. Put half of the avocados into a food processor or blender. Put the other half of the avocados into a medium-size bowl and mash with a fork.

2. Roughly chop half of the jalapeño and add it to the food processor. Mince the other half and add it to the bowl.

3. Add 1 tablespoon of the onion to the food processor. Add the remaining onion to the bowl. Blend the ingredients in the food processor until smooth, adding small amounts of water until the mixture is just pourable from a spoon. Pour the avocado mixture into the bowl with the other half of the ingredients and stir to incorporate. Add salt to taste.

4. Cover tightly with plastic wrap and refrigerate until ready to serve. If the surface of the salsa begins to darken, stir thoroughly before serving. The salsa will keep in the refrigerator for 1 to 2 days.

BAJA COLESLAW WITH SHRIMP
Ensalada de Col con Camarones

This decadent slaw recipe comes from chef Patricio Herrera, teacher of the Food of the Americas curriculum at the California Culinary Academy in San Francisco. It could stand alone as a taco filling on a wicked hot summer day. I recommend serving it as a crunchy, tangy counterpoint alongside any tacos. ***Note:*** *Other shellfish, such as lobster, crab, or sea urchin, can be substituted for the shrimp.*

MAKES 2 QUARTS (EIGHT 8-OUNCE SERVINGS, OR SIXTEEN 4-OUNCE SERVINGS)

> 1½ teaspoons cumin seeds
> 1½ teaspoons mild chili powder
> 7 tablespoons extra-virgin olive oil, divided
> 5 medium cloves garlic, minced, divided
> ½ pound raw medium shrimp, peeled and deveined (approximately 15 to 20)
> ½ cup chopped cilantro, divided
> Juice of 3 limes (approximately 6 tablespoons), divided
> Salt
> Freshly ground pepper
> ½ head green cabbage, cut finely into ribbons
> 1½ jalapeño chiles, seeded and finely chopped
> 3 medium tomatoes, cut into ¼-inch dice
> 3 avocados, peeled, pitted, and cut into ¼-inch dice
> 1 red onion, thinly sliced
> 5 tablespoons red wine vinegar

1. In a small cast-iron skillet or other heavy pan, toast the cumin seeds and chili powder, stirring constantly, until the chili powder just begins to change color, about 2 to 3 minutes. Immediately remove from the pan, and let cool on a small plate. Once cool, grind in a small electric spice mill. Set aside.

2. In a medium-size sauté pan, heat 1 tablespoon of the olive oil over medium-high heat. Add 1 clove of the minced garlic, the shrimp, 2 tablespoons of the cilantro, 2 tablespoons of the lime juice, and salt and pepper to taste, stirring frequently until the shrimp are just cooked through, about 3 minutes. Set aside on a plate to cool. When the shrimp have cooled, chop them into ¼-inch cubes.

3. In a large mixing bowl, combine the cabbage, jalapeños, tomatoes, avocados, onion, and red wine vinegar; the reserved cumin mixture; the reserved shrimp; and garlic, cilantro, lime juice, and olive oil. Add salt to taste. Refrigerate. Serve chilled.

TACO TIP

LIME-PICKLED RED ONIONS

Simple to make, these are an awesome taco condiment. Slice 1 large red onion into ¼-inch thick rounds. Break them up in a medium-size bowl and mix with 1 tablespoon salt. Let sit overnight. The next day, rinse them for about 3 minutes in a colander until they are just slightly salty to taste. Return onions to a clean bowl and add the juice of 2 limes (about 4 tablespoons). Mix well. Marinate for 1 hour before serving.

WHOLE PINTO BEANS
Frijoles de Olla

Beans are a staple throughout Mexico, and the pinto is undoubtedly the most famous. While most people know them in their "refried" form, pintos truly achieve sublime stature simmered to perfection in this simple broth. Fish them out with a slotted spoon for tacos, or serve them in bowls with some of the broth for a delicious soupy first course. Tender and toothsome, their mild pink flesh is deeply satisfying.

Variation: *To make black beans, omit the bacon and substitute one 6-inch sprig of fresh epazote for the bay leaf.*

MAKES 6 TO 7 CUPS OF BEANS

> 1 pound dried pinto beans (about 2¼ cups), picked over
> 3 slices of bacon, or a 4- to 6-ounce piece of pork fat
> ½ medium white onion, quartered
> 1 bay leaf (optional)
> Salt

1. Put the beans in a *cazuela* (a traditional Mexican clay pot), or a cast-iron or other heavy pot, and cover them with about 3 inches of water. Bring to a boil, then turn off the heat and cover. Let the beans sit for 1 hour, then add additional water if needed to cover the beans with 2 inches of water.

2. Meanwhile, fry the bacon over medium heat until it is slightly crispy, about 7 minutes. Remove from heat. Break the bacon into pieces and put it and its rendered fat into the pot with the beans. Add the onion and bay leaf, if using. Bring to a simmer and cook over medium-low heat, adding water as necessary to keep the beans covered, until the beans are soft, about 2 hours. Add salt to taste and serve.

RICE WITH VEGETABLES
Arroz con Verduras

Rice arrived in Mexico with the Spaniards five hundred years ago and soon began its fortunate partnership with beans as the dynamic duo of Mexican cooking (served with corn tortillas, of course). Mixed with butter and flecked with peas and corn, this simple rice dish pleases both the palate and the eye. Try it with handmade tortillas and Chile de Árbol Salsa (see page 6) for a really rootsy taco dinner.

MAKES ABOUT 7 CUPS

> 2 tablespoons olive oil
> ½ medium white onion, finely chopped
> 2 cups medium- or long-grain white rice
> 2 cups water
> 2 cups chicken or vegetable broth
> 1 to 1½ teaspoons salt
> 2 tablespoons unsalted butter
> ½ cup peas, fresh or frozen
> ½ cup sweet corn kernels, fresh off the cob or frozen

1. In a medium-size heavy-bottomed pot, add the oil and heat over medium heat. Add the onions and rice and sauté, stirring frequently, until the onions have turned lightly golden, about 10 minutes. Add the water, chicken broth, and salt. Turn the heat to very low, cover, and cook until all of the liquid is absorbed, about 20 minutes. Turn off the heat and leave the pot covered.

2. Meanwhile, in a small pan, melt the butter over medium heat and add the peas and corn, stirring occasionally until the vegetables are heated through, about 5 minutes.

3. Stir the vegetable mixture into the rice and serve.

ROASTED POBLANO CHILE STRIPS
Rajas de Chile Poblano

Deep green with medium heat, the comely poblano chile only gets better when roasted, which softens the flesh, helps to remove the skin, and concentrates the flavor, which is as deep as its color. To make roasting and peeling easier, choose poblanos that are as straight and smooth as possible.

MAKES ABOUT 12 POBLANO STRIPS

2 poblano chiles
1 teaspoon olive oil (if roasting on an electric range)

1. On a wood or charcoal grill, or directly over a medium-high flame on the grate of a gas range, place the poblanos and cook until the downward side has blackened, about 1 to 2 minutes. Turn the poblanos and repeat the process until all sides are blackened. If using an electric range, lightly coat the poblanos with the oil and place them in a preheated medium-size cast-iron pan over medium-high heat and blacken each side as much as possible. It may take a little longer than with the other methods of roasting.

2. Place the poblanos in a small metal or glass bowl and cover until cool enough to handle. Peel the poblanos and discard the skins. Black flecks will remain on the poblanos; do not rinse them. Then stem and seed the poblanos. For a milder flavor, devein them also. Tear the poblanos into strips about ½-inch wide, place them in a small bowl, and reserve.

3. To serve, place one or two poblano strips on top of each taco. Refrigerate leftovers in a covered container for up to a week.

PICKLED JALAPEÑOS AND CARROTS
Jalapeños y Zanahorias Encurtidos

Eating tacos at a taquería or taco truck without a jalapeño and a few spicy carrot rounds just doesn't seem right; it's not right at home, either. The cane vinegar makes for a more mellow liquid and is available in many supermarkets and international markets. A nod to Patricia Quintana for methodology and inspiration.

Note: *Plan ahead when making this dish, as the jalapeños and carrots need to pickle for at least two weeks.*

MAKES 2 QUARTS

> 12 large jalapeño chiles
> 1½ teaspoons coarse salt, divided
> 5 medium carrots, peeled and cut into ½-inch rounds
> ¼ cup olive oil
> 15 whole cloves garlic
> 2 medium white onions, cut into ¼-inch wedges
> 1 teaspoon dried marjoram
> ½ teaspoon whole black peppercorns
> 2 cups cider vinegar
> 2 cups cane vinegar
> Salt

1. Poke each jalapeño several times with a metal skewer or the tip of a sharp knife. Put enough water in a medium-size pot to cover the jalapeños, add 1 teaspoon of the salt, and bring to a gentle boil. Add the jalapeños and boil, uncovered, for 6 minutes. Turn off the heat, let the jalapeños sit in the water for 4 minutes, uncovered, then remove them with a slotted spoon and let cool. Reserve half of the water.

2. Meanwhile, bring small pot of water to a boil, add the remaining salt and the carrots, and cook until slightly soft, but still crunchy, about 6 minutes. Remove the carrots with a slotted spoon and let cool.

3. In a large *cazuela* (a traditional Mexican clay pot), or deep cast-iron or enamel pot, heat the oil over medium-high heat. Add the garlic and onions, stirring rapidly so that they stay crunchy, and sauté until lightly browned, about 5 minutes. Add the marjoram, peppercorns, cider vinegar, cane vinegar, reserved jalapeño water, and salt to taste.

4. Cover the pot and bring to a boil. Remove the lid, add the reserved jalapeños and carrots, and bring to a boil again. Turn off the heat and let cool.

5. Distribute the jalapeño mixture and cooking liquid evenly between 2 sterilized glass quart jars, packing in the vegetables first, then adding the liquid afterward.

6. Let the jars sit in the refrigerator for 2 weeks before using. Remove the jalapeños, carrots, and onions as needed to accompany tacos. They will keep in the refrigerator for several months.

PICKLED CHIPOTLES
Chipotles á la Poblana

Chipotles are smoke-dried jalapeños. This recipe from the Mexican state of Puebla, adapted from Patricia Quintana's *La cocina de Los Angeles*, is refreshingly different from the ubiquitous canned iteration. You can use dried chipotles or *moritas*, found in Mexican markets or online. This recipe calls for *piloncillo*, small cones of unrefined solid cane sugar, but you can substitute dark brown sugar if piloncillo is unavailable.

Note: *Plan ahead when making this dish, as the chipotles need to pickle for at least two weeks.*

MAKES 1 TO 2 QUARTS

> One 4-ounce package dried chipotle chiles (about 40 chiles)
> 1 teaspoon salt
> 3 tablespoons olive oil
> 1 large white onion, cut into quarters
> 1 head garlic, skin on, cut in half through the middle of the cloves
> 1 bay leaf

¼ teaspoon dried thyme
¼ teaspoon dried marjoram
¼ teaspoon whole black peppercorns
4 medium carrots, peeled and cut into ½-inch rounds
¾ cup cider vinegar
4 ounces piloncillo, or ½ cup dark brown sugar, dissolved in ¼ cup water

1. Poke each chipotle several times with a metal skewer or the tip of a sharp knife. In a large pot, cover them well with water and add the salt. Bring the water to a boil, then turn off immediately, stirring once to make sure the salt is incorporated into the water. Adjust salt if necessary. Let cool uncovered, then cover and let soak for 1 day. Remove the chipotles with a slotted spoon and reserve them in a bowl.

2. In a large *cazuela* (a traditional Mexican clay pot), or deep cast-iron or enamel pot, heat the oil over medium heat. Add the onions and garlic, stirring frequently, until onions are lightly golden, about 5 minutes. Add the bay leaf, thyme, marjoram, and peppercorns, stirring for 1 minute. Add the reserved chipotles, stirring for 1 minute. Add the carrots, vinegar, and the piloncillo/water mixture.

3. Bring the contents to a boil, then stir rapidly to break the boil. Repeat two more times. Turn off the heat and let the pot cool, uncovered.

4. Distribute the chipotle mixture and cooking liquid evenly between 2 sterilized glass quart jars.

5. Let the jars sit in the refrigerator for 2 weeks before using. Remove chipotles, carrots, and onions as needed to accompany tacos. They will keep in the refrigerator for several months.

STRANGE BUT WONDERFUL TACOS

What's the strangest filling that you can imagine going into a taco? Does the idea of eating a beef tongue freak you out? How about a tortilla loaded up with grasshoppers?

Since the dawn of the tortilla, Mesoamericans have been filling it with just about everything imaginable. Pre-Hispanic staples included not only numerous vegetables, herbs, seeds, mushrooms, fish, amphibians, crustaceans, and fowl, but also worms and even a hairless dog called the *xoloizcuintle*. Many of these are still sold today, mainly in southern Mexico.

I always try a new taco if I see it on the menu. This has led me to order *tacos de ojo* (beef eyeball), *labio* (beef lips), *cachete* (beef cheek), *sesos* (beef brain), *cuerito* (pigskin simmered in lard), *buche* (pig stomach), and *birria de chivo con chicharrones* (stewed goat with deep-fried pigskins crumbled on top—for breakfast, no less!).

If you're really adventurous, keep an eye out for *tacos de trompa* (pig snout). Don't mistake them for *trompo*, which is marinated pork (*al pastor*) cooked on a vertical spit, a filling with Middle Eastern origins that arrived in Mexico between the 1930s and 1950s, depending on what story you believe. Look out for these other delicacies as well: *bofe* (lung), *oreja* (ear), *higado* (liver), *corazón* (heart), *nana* (uterus), *pajarilla* (pancreas), *paloma* (dove), *machita* (lamb testicle), *moronga* (blood sausage), and the ingenious combinations of *chanfaina* (lung, heart, and liver) and *nenepil* (cheek and uterus).

At Tacos Beto in Mexico City, the specialty is the *taco de cochinada*, a term that translates roughly as "filth," and is appropriately composed of remains from the bottom of the fryer. The Web site Chilango.com describes it as "a toxic delicacy for crude palates. There is no underground gourmet that doesn't know this temple of seedy gastronomy."

As you can see, there are apparently no limits when it comes to taco fillings, so long as the filling can stay inside the tortilla long enough for you to eat it. Unless, of course, you're making a *taco de nada*—a nothing taco—in which case you simply warm the tortilla, roll it up, and enjoy!

TACOS

Tacos de Canasta
Scrambled Egg Taco with Poblano Strips
Potato and Chorizo Taco

Tacos de Cazuela
Coffee and Chile–Braised Beef Brisket Taco
Beef Tongue Taco
Beef Meatball Taco in Guajillo Sauce
La Esquina's Achiote and Citrus–Marinated Pork Taco
La Esquina's Chicken in Tomato and Chipotle Sauce
Spice-Rubbed Chicken Thigh Taco
Braised Chard and Cheese Taco
Winter Squash Taco with Coriander-Cumin Crema
Duck Breast Taco in Pumpkin Seed Sauce
Pork Loin in Chile Adobo with Grilled Pineapple

Tacos al Carbón
Grilled Beef Flap Steak Taco
Grilled Chicken Breast Taco
Taco El Perrón

Tacos de Sartén
Baja Fish Taco
Shrimp and Sofrito Taco
Spiced Ground Turkey Taco
Garlic–Wild Mushroom Taco with Creamed Corn and Morita Salsa

Tacos Dorados
Zucchini and Cheese Taco Dorado
Chorizo and Cactus Taco Dorado
Fish and Sofrito Taco Dorado

SCRAMBLED EGG TACO
WITH POBLANO STRIPS
Taco de Huevo Revuelto con Rajas

All over Mexico, *tacos de canasta*, or "basket" tacos, are sold on the streets in the morning to busy workers of all classes. With deep green poblano strips and spicy red salsa gracing the yellow mound of fluffy eggs, these tacos are one of my favorite breakfast dishes (though they're delicious at any time of day). The *queso fresco*, or fresh cheese, in this and other recipes is crumbly and slightly acidic. A very mild feta cheese is a suitable substitute.

MAKES 6 TACOS

Corn or flour tortillas

Filling

6 eggs
Salt
Freshly ground pepper
2 tablespoons olive oil
½ medium white onion, finely chopped

Suggested toppings

Roasted Poblano Chile Strips (see page 22)
Sierra-Style Tomato Salsa (see page 3)
¼ pound queso fresco, crumbled

1. In a medium-size bowl, whisk the eggs until well blended. Add salt and pepper to taste. Heat a medium-size cast-iron pan over medium heat. Add the olive oil and tilt the pan to coat the bottom. Add the onion and sauté until soft, about 4 minutes. Add the eggs to the pan and stir gently while cooking until the eggs are just cooked through, about 7 minutes.

2. Serve on warm corn or flour tortillas, topped with a couple of poblano strips, Sierra-Style Tomato Salsa, and crumbled queso fresco.

POTATO AND CHORIZO TACO
Taco de Papa y Chorizo

Mexican chorizo is different from Spanish chorizo, which is a cured product. The best Mexican chorizo comes house-made from Mexican markets, redolent of herbs and spices and bright red from *achiote*, the subtle and earthy-flavored seed of the tropical annatto tree. Try to avoid the cheap chorizo that comes in plastic casing, as it usually contains low-quality meat and a very high percentage of fat that renders out during cooking.

MAKES 12 TACOS

Filling

    ½ pound medium russet or white potatoes, quartered
    1 tablespoon olive oil
    ¼ pound Mexican chorizo in bite-size pieces, removed from casing
    ¼ medium white onion, cut in ¼-inch wedges
    Corn or flour tortillas

Suggested toppings

    La Esquina Taquería's Green Salsa (see page 12)
    Chopped onion and cilantro
    Limes, cut into wedges

1. Put the potatoes in a medium-size pot and cover them with water. Bring the water almost to a boil, then lower it to a simmer, cooking the potatoes until barely tender, between 10 to 15 minutes. Be sure not to overcook them potatoes. Drain the potatoes and put them on a plate to cool. Once they are cool, cut them into ½-inch cubes.

2. Meanwhile, heat a medium-size pan over medium heat and add the olive oil. Tilt the pan to coat the bottom, and add the onion, cooking until translucent, about 5 to 7 minutes. Add the chorizo and sauté, stirring occasionally, for 7 to 10 minutes more, until cooked through. Add the potatoes and stir in gently. Cook until the potatoes are warmed through, about 5 more minutes.

3. Serve on warm corn or flour tortillas, topped with Cooked Tomatillo Salsa and chopped onion and cilantro, with lime wedges on the side.

COFFEE AND CHILE–BRAISED BEEF BRISKET TACO

Taco de Machaca Estilo Momocho

Tacos de cazuela, their fillings simmered in pots, are widespread throughout Mexico. Often, the *cazuela*, or pot, is placed on the table, and each person fills his or her own tortillas. This recipe comes from Eric Williams, the chef and owner of Momocho in Cleveland and one of the top chefs in the country exploring modern Mexican cuisine. This brisket recipe is easy to make, but the result is deep and heartwarming—so good, in fact, that you will be happy to have leftovers. Just reheat some of the meat and liquid and spread it onto a nice piece of baguette, top with onions and cilantro, and you have an awesome lunch or dinner for the next day. To make ancho chile powder, just break a few dried ancho chiles into small pieces and grind them in a small spice grinder.

MAKES 12 TO 15 TACOS

Corn tortillas

Filling

2 tablespoons ancho chile powder

½ teaspoon ground cinnamon

2 tablespoons freshly ground Guatemalan coffee, medium to full roast, or another medium-roasted coffee

3 tablespoons kosher salt; divided

2½ pounds beef brisket, quartered and trimmed of excess fat

½ cup red wine vinegar

¾ cup unseasoned tomato juice

Juice from 2 limes (approximately 4 tablespoons)

1 cup red wine

½ tablespoon freshly ground pepper

1 bay leaf

½ medium Spanish or yellow onion, peeled and quartered

Suggested toppings

Fresh Tomatillo Salsa (see page 10)

Chunky Guacamole (see page 14)

¼ pound *queso fresco*, crumbled
Limes, cut into wedges

1. In a small bowl, mix the ancho chile powder, cinnamon, coffee, and 2 tablespoons of the salt together. Rub the seasoning all over the surface of the brisket pieces and place them on a large plate or baking sheet. On a grill, or in a large cast-iron pan over medium-high heat, sear the seasoned brisket, 4 to 5 minutes per side. It should smell toasty as the spices caramelize, but not burned.

2. In a braising pan or heavy-bottomed Dutch oven, or other heavy pot, add the brisket, vinegar, tomato juice, lime juice, wine, the remaining salt, the pepper, bay leaf, and onion.

3. Add enough water to cover the brisket, cover the pan, and place it on the stove. Bring to a boil, then lower the heat and simmer, covered, for 3 hours or until the brisket is tender. Remove the bay leaf and onion and discard. Remove the meat and shred it, reserving the cooking liquid.

4. Serve on warm corn tortillas, topped with Fresh Tomatillo Salsa, Chunky Guacamole, and crumbled queso fresco, with lime wedges on the side. To reheat any leftovers, put the meat and reserved cooking liquid in a pot and warm over medium-low heat, stirring frequently, until hot. If reheating in a microwave, warm the meat and liquid 30 seconds at a time, stirring in between, until hot.

BEEF TONGUE TACO
Taco de Lengua

Strange to some, tongue tacos are standard fare at taquerías. I love the tongue in a spicy tomato sauce that a restaurant in my hometown used to serve. I've attempted to re-create it here with the Chipotle Salsa Ranchera below. For a mild version, warm the diced tongue in Fresh Tomatillo Salsa (see page 10) instead. For more adventurous eaters, this recipe is the perfect anchor for a *taquiza*, a taco party.

MAKES 10 TO 14 TACOS

Corn tortillas

Filling

1 small beef tongue, about 2 pounds
1 medium white onion, quartered, divided
4 cloves garlic, peeled, divided
4 whole black peppercorns
1 small bay leaf
½ teaspoon dried thyme
½ teaspoon dried marjoram
2½ teaspoons salt, divided
8 medium tomatoes (about 2 pounds)
3 *chipotles en adobo*
2 tablespoons olive oil

Suggested toppings

Chopped onion and cilantro
Limes, cut into wedges

1. For the filling, in a medium-size pot, put the tongue, 3 of the onion quarters, 2 cloves of the garlic, the peppercorns, bay leaf, thyme, marjoram, and 2 teaspoons of the salt, and add enough water to cover. Bring to a boil, then simmer, covered, for 3 hours, turning the tongue over after 1½ hours and adding more water as necessary to keep the tongue covered. Let the tongue cool in the broth.

2. Remove the tongue from the broth and cut off the small bones at the base. Slice through the skin on top of the tongue, lengthwise from base to tip, then peel the skin off. Inspect the tongue, especially the underside, and cut off any fat. Chop the tongue into ¼-inch cubes. Put them in a bowl, cover with some of the broth, and refrigerate until ready to use.

3. For the Chipotle Salsa Ranchera, on a cast-iron griddle or in a large cast-iron pan over medium-high heat, cook the tomatoes, turning every minute or so, until they are softened and have brown marks, about 5 minutes. Let cool. Meanwhile, roughly chop the remaining garlic. Put the tomatoes, garlic, and chipotles in a food processor or blender, and pulse until the ingredients are incorporated but still chunky.

4. In a medium-size pan, heat the oil over medium heat. Finely chop the remaining onion, add to the pan, and cook until softened, about 5 minutes. Add the tomato mixture and the remaining salt to the pan and cook over high heat, stirring frequently with a metal or wooden spatula until the sauce thickens, about 10 to 15 minutes. Scrape the pan frequently as the sauce thickens to prevent scorching.

5. To assemble, first heat the chipotle salsa ranchera in a large pot over medium heat, stirring frequently. Remove the tongue pieces from the broth with a slotted spoon and add them to the salsa, discarding the broth. Continue cooking for 15 to 20 minutes, or until the meat is heated through. If the sauce thickens and begins to stick to the pot, add a little water to thin it.

6. Serve on warm corn tortillas, topped with chopped onion and cilantro, with lime wedges on the side.

BEEF MEATBALL TACO IN GUAJILLO SAUCE

Albondigas de Res en Salsa de Guajillo

I forget how much kids love meatballs until I serve these. Grown-up kids love them, too. Use a pan large enough to fit all of the meatballs—they *will* get eaten. This recipe was inspired by and adapted from various recipes in Diana Kennedy's *The Cuisines of Mexico*.

MAKES 12 TACOS

Corn or flour tortillas

Filling

4 *guajillo* chiles
6 medium tomatoes (about 1½ pounds)
½ white onion, cut into quarters
2 cloves garlic
2 teaspoons salt, divided
¼ cup olive oil
1 egg
1 pound lean ground beef
1 small zucchini, minced (about 1 cup)
¼ teaspoon dried oregano
¼ teaspoon freshly ground pepper
¼ teaspoon ground cumin

Suggested toppings

Tomatillo and Chile de Árbol Salsa (see page 13)
¼ pound Cotija cheese, crumbled
Chopped onion and cilantro
Limes, cut into wedges

1. For the sauce, stem, seed, and break the guajillos into pieces. Put them in a medium-size bowl and cover them with boiling water. Cover the bowl and let sit until the guajillos have softened, about 30 minutes. Remove the guajillos with a slotted spoon and set aside.

2. Meanwhile, on a *comal* or medium-size cast-iron pan over medium heat, roast the tomatoes, onion, and garlic, turning them, until they are softened and have brown marks, about 10 minutes. Remove from heat, let cool slightly, and coarsely chop. In a food processor or blender, combine the guajillos, tomatoes, onion, garlic, and 1 teaspoon of the salt, and pulse until incorporated but still chunky.

3. In a large pan, heat the olive oil over medium heat. Add the sauce and cook, stirring, for 10 to 15 minutes.

4. For the meatballs, in a small bowl, beat the egg. In a medium-size bowl, combine the ground beef, zucchini, oregano, pepper, cumin, and the remaining salt. Mix well with your hands. Add the egg and continue to mix with your hands until it is very well incorporated.

5. Lower the sauce to low heat. With a soup spoon, scoop about 2 tablespoons of the meatball mix and form into a ball. Repeat the process to make 36 balls. Place the meatballs in the sauce, one by one, close together. Spoon some of the sauce over the meatballs, cover the pan, and cook on low. Stir gently after about 20 minutes, cover the pot again, and finish cooking, about 10 more minutes.

6. Serve 3 meatballs on each warm corn or flour tortilla, topped with Tomatillo and Chile de Árbol Salsa, crumbled Cotija cheese, and chopped onion and cilantro, with lime wedges on the side.

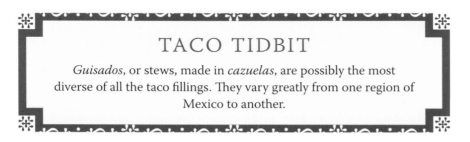

TACO TIDBIT

Guisados, or stews, made in *cazuelas*, are possibly the most diverse of all the taco fillings. They vary greatly from one region of Mexico to another.

LA ESQUINA'S ACHIOTE AND CITRUS–MARINATED PORK TACO

Cochinita Pibil Estilo La Esquina

This recipe comes from chef Jose Alvarado from New York City's La Esquina. This is one of his favorite tacos. Traditionally, this dish is prepared in a *pib*, or a Mayan pit oven. Here, we use a regular oven, and the process is a bit involved, but the results are staggering. This is a perfect dish for a big taco party with friends and family. The *achiote* paste and seeds are available in Latin American markets.

MAKES 12 TO 16 TACOS

Corn tortillas

Filling

2 tablespoons achiote seeds

Juice of 2 lemons (about 6 tablespoons)

Juice of 1½ oranges (about 7 tablespoons)

Juice of 1 grapefruit (about 11 tablespoons)

2 tablespoons plus 1½ teaspoons balsamic vinegar

1½ teaspoons plus ⅜ teaspoon ground allspice

2¼ teaspoons dried Mexican oregano

⅜ teaspoon ground cloves, plus 1 whole clove

2 pounds pork butt meat, trimmed of fat and cut into 2-inch cubes

1 small tomato, chopped, plus 1 small tomato, quartered

¼ medium yellow onion, chopped, plus ½ medium yellow onion, cut into ¼-inch slices

5 tablespoons achiote paste

1½ teaspoons white balsamic vinegar

Juice of ½ lime (about 1 tablespoon)

Zest of ½ lime

1 clove garlic, minced

⅜ teaspoon ground coriander

¼ teaspoon freshly ground pepper

½ bay leaf

Salt

Suggested toppings
> Pickled Jalapeños and Carrots (see page 23)
> Lime-Pickled Red Onions (see page 18)
> Shredded green cabbage

1. For the marinade, in a food processor or blender, combine the achiote seed, lemon juice, 5 tablespoons of the orange juice, 10 tablespoons of the grapefruit juice, 2 tablespoons of the balsamic vinegar, 1½ teaspoons of the allspice, 1½ teaspoons of the oregano, and the ground cloves. Blend until smooth.

2. Put the pork pieces in a large pan, pour the marinade over them, and refrigerate overnight.

3. For the adobo, combine the chopped tomato, chopped onion, achiote paste, the remaining 2 tablespoons orange juice, the remaining 1 tablespoon grapefruit juice, the white balsamic vinegar, lime juice, lime zest, garlic, the remaining ⅜ teaspoon allspice, the coriander, the remaining ¾ teaspoon Mexican oregano, the whole clove, and the pepper. In a food processor or blender, blend in two batches until smooth.

4. Preheat the oven to 350°F.

5. Place the marinated pork butt in a large Dutch oven or other large, heavy pot. To finish the adobo, add the bay leaves, the quartered tomato, the sliced onion, the remaining 1½ teaspoons balsamic vinegar, and salt to taste. Pour the adobo mixture over the pork and stir to combine. Heat the pot over medium heat until the contents come to a simmer. Cover and place in the oven. Braise for 2 to 3 hours, or until the pork is fork-tender. Shred the chunks of meat.

6. Serve on warm corn tortillas, topped with Pickled Jalapeños and Carrots, Lime-Pickled Red Onions, and shredded cabbage.

LA ESQUINA'S CHICKEN IN TOMATO AND CHIPOTLE SAUCE

Tinga de Pollo Estilo La Esquina Taquería

Chicken *tinga* is great for using leftover chicken. At La Esquina, they spit-roast the chicken whole, then shred it and add it to the tomato mixture. Serve the tinga on warm corn tortillas with shredded cabbage, sliced avocado, and chipotle salsa (included here). This recipe calls for "sweating" the onions—sautéing them covered over low heat until they are very soft.

MAKES 12 TACOS

Corn or flour tortillas

Filling

2 tablespoons olive oil
1½ medium yellow onions, cut into ⅛-inch rounds, plus ¼ medium
  yellow onion, diced
7 medium tomatoes
2 to 4 *chipotles en adobo*, puréed
1½ pounds chicken, cooked and shredded
Salt
Freshly ground pepper
1 small clove garlic, minced
½ teaspoon sugar

Suggested toppings

Shredded green cabbage
Avocado slices

1. For the chicken, in a medium-size pan with a lid, over low heat, warm 1 tablespoon of the olive oil. Add the onion rounds to the oil, cover, and sweat them, stirring occasionally until soft, about 20 minutes. Add ½ of the chipotle purée and cook for 30 minutes, covered. Cut 5 of the tomatoes into quarters and add them to the pan, cooking for an additional 30 minutes. Add the cooked chicken and stir to combine. Simmer until the chicken is thoroughly heated through, about 10 minutes.

2. For the salsa, on a grill, or in a medium-size cast-iron pan, over medium-high heat, cook the remaining 2 whole tomatoes, moving frequently, until they are softened and have brown marks, about 10 minutes. Remove from the grill or pan and set aside.

3. In a medium-size pan over medium heat, sauté the diced onion and the garlic in the remaining 1 tablespoon oil until they are fragrant, about 2 minutes. Place them in a food processor or blender with the charred tomatoes, the remaining puréed chipotles, the sugar, and ⅛ cup of water. Purée until smooth. Add salt to taste.

4. Serve the chicken on warm corn or flour tortillas, topped with the chipotle salsa, shredded cabbage, and avocado slices.

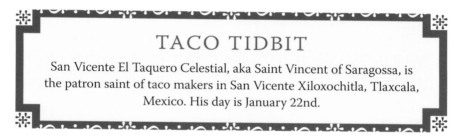

TACO TIDBIT

San Vicente El Taquero Celestial, aka Saint Vincent of Saragossa, is the patron saint of taco makers in San Vicente Xiloxochitla, Tlaxcala, Mexico. His day is January 22nd.

THROWING A TAQUIZA

A *taquiza* is a taco party. In her book *Jergas de Habla Hispana*, Roxana Fitch defines a taquiza as a meal based on a great variety or huge quantities of tacos. Sounds good. One example she gives is, "*Conozco una lonchería aquí cerquita donde podemos echarnos una buena taquiza,*" which translates to something like, "I know a lunch place nearby where we can throw down a bunch of tacos."

Throwing your own taquiza is fun and fairly easy with some advance planning. First, choose the number and type of fillings. *Cazuela*-style fillings (anything served in a pot), such as Coffee and Chile–Braised Beef Brisket (see page 33) or Braised Chard and Cheese (see page 48) can be made ahead and reheated in the oven just before serving. Grilled fillings, like Grilled Beef Flap Steak (see page 57) and Grilled Chicken Breast (see page 60), can be cooked to order. Count on about 2 ounces of meat per taco. You should be safe planning on two or three tacos per person if there are also some side dishes; three or four if there aren't.

Second, make your salsas. You can make as many salsas as you choose, but the minimum would be one hot salsa (usually a red variety) and one mild (usually tomatillo-based).

Third, decide on accompaniments. If you're grilling, grilled onions—either Mexican *cebolletas* or thick rounds of white onions—and jalapeños are a must. Also mandatory are chopped white onion and cilantro, Pickled Jalapeños and Carrots (see page 23), fresh whole radishes, and lime wedges.

Warm the tortillas just before service and place them in a tortilla warmer or inside a linen cloth in a bowl with a lid. If you are serving flour tortillas, find the smallest size possible. This is a taco party, not a burrito feed! Many places make their tacos with double corn tortillas—it prevents the tacos from breaking up midbite. Instruct your guests about this and buy plenty of tortillas.

And don't forget the drinks. *Aguas frescas* are a must, as is a cooler filled with Mexican beer and soda pop. Serve the aguas frescas in big glass jars with ladles. Make extra to freeze as ice cubes, then add them to the chilled aguas frescas just before serving.

SPICE-RUBBED CHICKEN THIGH TACO

Taco de Pollo en Recado

Chicken breast always steals the spotlight, but in this recipe, the dark, moist thigh is the star. Rubbed with a Rick Bayless– and Yucatán-inspired *recado* (an *achiote*-based spice blend) and baked in the oven, the meat falls right off the bone and into your waiting tortilla.

MAKES 12 TACOS

Corn or flour tortillas

Filling

¼ cup bitter orange juice, or 3 tablespoons orange juice
  plus 1 tablespoon white vinegar
1 tablespoon water
2 tablespoons achiote seeds or achiote paste
¼ teaspoon cumin seeds
¼ teaspoon dried oregano
¼ teaspoon dried thyme
8 whole black peppercorns
3 whole allspice berries
¼ teaspoon paprika
4 cloves garlic, roughly chopped
1 teaspoon salt
1 tablespoon toasted sesame seeds
2 pounds chicken thighs (about 4 large thighs)

Suggested toppings

Fresh Tomato Salsa (see page 2)
Avocado Crema (see page 47)
Chopped onion and cilantro
Limes, cut into wedges

1. For the recado, in a food processor or blender, combine the orange juice, water, achiote seed, cumin, oregano, thyme, peppercorns, allspice, paprika,

garlic, and salt. Blend until smooth. Pour the mixture into a medium-size bowl and stir in the sesame seeds.

2. Add the chicken thighs to the bowl, turning to coat them well with the recado. Cover the bowl and refrigerate for at least 4 hours, or ideally overnight.

3. Preheat the oven to 350°F.

4. In a pot or oven-safe pan with a lid, place the thighs, well-coated with the recado; cover, and bake for 50 minutes. Uncover the pot, raise the heat to 400°F, and bake for 10 more minutes, or until the skin is crisp and the meat is cooked through. When checking for doneness, remember that thigh meat is dark, and the meat may appear reddish even when done.

5. Remove the chicken thighs from the pot and shred the meat. Be sure to include the skin. Serve on warm corn or flour tortillas, topped with Fresh Tomato Salsa, Avocado Crema, and chopped onion and cilantro, with lime wedges on the side.

TACO TIP

Avocado Crema is a delicious gestalt. Blend one avocado with ½ to 1 cup Mexican Crema (page 10) and serve with your favorite tacos.

BRAISED CHARD AND CHEESE TACO
Taco de Acelgas con Queso

Chard is underrated. It may be unassuming when raw, but when it's braised for a long time, it becomes a tender and sublime affair. Melt some cheese over it and you have a delectable taco filling. Deborah Madison's *Vegetarian Cooking for Everyone* inspired my creation of this recipe.

MAKES 12 TACOS

Corn or flour tortillas

Filling

2 large bunches chard (about 2 pounds), stemmed (stems reserved) and
cut roughly into 1- by 2-inch pieces
1 medium white onion, diced
½ cup cilantro, chopped
¼ cup olive oil
¼ teaspoon cayenne (optional)
¾ teaspoon paprika
2 cloves garlic, chopped
½ teaspoon salt
¼ cup water
¼ teaspoon freshly ground pepper
¼ pound Oaxaca or mozzarella cheese, grated

Suggested topping

Chile de Árbol Salsa (see page 6)

1. Chop half of the reserved chard stems into ¼-inch pieces and combine in a deep cast-iron or other heavy pot with the chard, onion, cilantro, olive oil, cayenne, paprika, garlic, salt, water, and pepper to taste. Mix well and cook, covered, over low heat for 45 minutes, adding more water at intervals if there is less than ½ inch of water on the bottom of the pot.

2. Preheat the oven to 400°F.

3. Uncover the pot and remove it from the heat. Once the steam has dissipated, stir the vegetables and, with tongs or a slotted spoon, quickly

transfer the chard mixture to an oven-safe pan or dish. Sprinkle the cheese over the chard and bake it in the oven until the cheese is melted and lightly browned, about 5 to 10 minutes.

4. To serve, remove some chard and cheese with tongs, let drain, and put on warm corn or flour tortillas, topped with Chile de Árbol Salsa.

TACO TIP

During winter, kale is at its peak, sweet and nutritious. Consider substituting some or all of the chard in the Braised Chard and Cheese Taco recipe with kale.

WINTER SQUASH TACO WITH CORIANDER-CUMIN CREMA

Taco de Calabaza con Crema Mexicana

After we've harvested the winter squash in early autumn, our family meal plan fills with numerous squash dishes, including our own invention: squash tacos. They're rich and nourishing with crema on top. Think creamy squash soup in a tortilla. The filling gets very little treatment, so use delicata, acorn, or another sweeter squash. Mash in the roasted garlic and you're ready to go.

MAKES 12 TACOS

Corn or flour tortillas

Filling

1 acorn squash or 2 delicata squash (about 1½ pounds)
1 teaspoon olive oil
Salt
Freshly ground pepper
1 head garlic, skin on, cut in half through the middle of the cloves
1 cup Mexican Crema (see page 10)
⅛ teaspoon ground cumin
⅛ teaspoon ground coriander
Pinch of cinnamon

Suggested toppings

Tomatillo and Chile de Árbol Salsa (see page 13)
Chopped cilantro

1. Preheat the oven to 350°F.

2. Cut the squash in half and scoop out the seeds. Rub the inside and cut edges of each squash half with the olive oil. Season lightly with salt and pepper.

3. Place the squash on a baking sheet, cut side down, with a garlic piece under each half. Bake for about 50 minutes, or until soft.

4. For the coriander-cumin crema, while the squash is baking, combine the Mexican Crema, cumin, coriander, and cinnamon in a small pot and warm over low heat for 10 minutes. Set aside.

5. Remove the squash from the oven and let cool slightly. Scoop squash into a medium-size bowl and partially mash with a fork. Squeeze the garlic out of its skin into the bowl, and mash it into the squash. Season to taste with salt and pepper.

6. Serve on warm corn or flour tortillas, topped with the coriander-cumin crema, Tomatillo and Chile de Árbol Salsa, and cilantro.

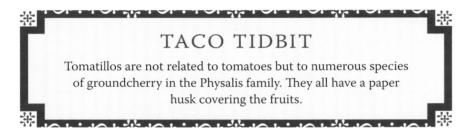

TACO TIDBIT

Tomatillos are not related to tomatoes but to numerous species of groundcherry in the Physalis family. They all have a paper husk covering the fruits.

DUCK BREAST TACO IN PUMPKIN SEED SAUCE
Taco de Pato en Pipián Verde

Puebla and Oaxaca are famous for their *pipiáns* and moles. These puréed sauces range from fairly simple to quite elaborate. Historically, pre-Hispanic pipiáns (also spelled pepián) used pumpkin seeds for thickening, though nowadays they might contain different seeds or nuts. This sauce hits the mark with its pumpkin seed base, drizzled over pan-fried duck breasts.

MAKES 12 TACOS

> Corn or flour tortillas

Filling

> 10 ounces raw pumpkin seeds, about 2¼ cups
> 1 cup chicken or vegetable broth, plus more if needed
> ¼ cup cilantro leaves, plus more for garnish
> 5 serrano chiles, roughly chopped (use less for a milder version)
> 1 medium white onion, roughly chopped
> 1 clove garlic, roughly chopped
> 4 leaves green-leaf lettuce
> 2 tablespoons vegetable oil or lard
> Five 5-ounce duck breasts, skin on
> Salt
> Freshly ground pepper

Suggested toppings

> Chile de Árbol Salsa (see page 6)
> Mexican Crema (see page 10)
> Toasted pumpkin seeds

1. In a medium-size cast-iron or other heavy pan over low heat, toast the pumpkin seeds until they begin to pop, being careful not to burn them.

2. For the pipián, in a food processor or blender, combine 1¾ cups of the pumpkin seeds, chicken broth, cilantro, serranos, onion, garlic, and lettuce.

Blend until smooth. Add more broth, if necessary, until the blend is easily pourable.

3. In a medium-size pan over high heat, heat the oil and fry the pumpkin seed mixture until it bubbles, stirring frequently, about 5 minutes. Remove from heat.

4. Heat a medium-size pan over medium-high heat for a few minutes. While it's heating, season the skin side of the duck breasts with salt and pepper. Place the breasts in the pan, skin side down, and agitate the pan until the fat begins to render so that the skin doesn't stick. Turn the heat down to medium and cook the breasts for 12 to 15 minutes, until all the fat is rendered and the skin is crisp.

5. Remove the breasts from the pan and pour off the fat. Return the breasts to the pan, meat side down, and cook for 30 to 45 seconds, until medium rare to medium.

6. Place the breasts on a cutting board, cut them into medallions, and place the medallions on warm corn or flour tortillas, topped with hot pipián. Serve immediately with Chile de Árbol Salsa, Mexican Crema, and the remaining toasted pumpkin seeds.

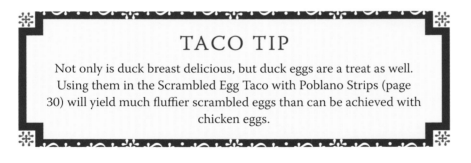

TACO TIP

Not only is duck breast delicious, but duck eggs are a treat as well. Using them in the Scrambled Egg Taco with Poblano Strips (page 30) will yield much fluffier scrambled eggs than can be achieved with chicken eggs.

PORK LOIN IN CHILE ADOBO WITH GRILLED PINEAPPLE

Carne Enchilada con Piña Asada

At La Esquina Taquería in New York, chef Jose Alvarado says his Carne Enchilada Tacos are a favorite among the regulars. Three types of dried chiles give the adobo a unique taste. Serve with warm corn tortillas, chopped fresh cilantro, grilled pineapple, and La Esquina Taquería's Green Salsa.

MAKES 12 TACOS

Corn tortillas

Filling

2 small dried *guajillo* chiles, stemmed

1 dried ancho chile, stemmed

½ to 1 dried chipotle chile, stemmed

1 clove garlic, roughly chopped

1 tablespoon cider vinegar

1 tablespoon water

1 whole clove, toasted and ground

⅛ teaspoon dried oregano

⅛ teaspoon cumin seeds, toasted and ground

¾ teaspoon sugar

1 plum tomato

Salt

Freshly ground pepper

1½ pounds boneless pork loin, trimmed of most of the fat

½ pineapple, peeled, cored and cut into ¾-inch-thick rounds

Suggested toppings

Chopped cilantro

La Esquina Taquería's Green Salsa (see page 12)

Grilled pineapple

1. In a medium-size pan over medium heat, toast the guajillos, ancho, and chipotle. Put them in a small bowl or pot and pour boiling water over

them to cover. Cover the bowl and let the chiles sit until softened, about 30 minutes.

2. In a food processor or blender, combine the chiles, garlic, vinegar, water, clove, oregano, cumin, sugar, and tomato. Blend until smooth. Season with salt and pepper to taste.

3. Rub the purée all over the pork loin. Allow to marinate in the refrigerator for at least 2 hours. On a barbecue or in a grill pan, grill the pork loin, turning occasionally, until cooked through, about 20 to 25 minutes, and dice into bite-size pieces.

4. When the pork is nearly done, grill the pineapple rounds on a barbecue or in a grill pan until lightly charred, about 3 to 4 minutes per side. Cut them into ¼- to ½-inch cubes and put them in a serving bowl.

5. Serve the pork loin on warm corn tortillas, topped with chopped cilantro, La Esquina Taquería's Green Salsa, and grilled pineapple.

TACO TIP

Dried chipotle chiles are increasingly available in stores, sold in 1- to 4-ounce packets. Also look for moritas, which are smoked, dried chiles. Don't be afraid to rehydrate one or two, and toss them into any salsa that you fancy.

GRILLED BEEF FLAP STEAK TACO
Taco de Carne Asada al Carbón

Al carbón means cooked over charcoal (preferably mesquite). In northern Mexico, the meats are usually sliced thin and cooked fast over hot coals, searing in the juices. The best *carne asada al carbón* tacos I've ever had come from Los Amigos Taquería in Tecate, Baja California Norte. There they serve nothing but asada, with marinated steaks sizzling on the grills, smoke billowing from the stovepipes, and guys whacking the meat into bite-size pieces with a cleaver in each hand. My inspiration from them: Serve it sizzling hot, right off the grill. The *preparada* (spice blend) I've included here is based on the one sold at my local Mexican butcher shop.

MAKES 16 TACOS

Corn or flour tortillas

Filling

3 tablespoons paprika
½ teaspoon ground cumin
½ teaspoon dried thyme
½ teaspoon dried oregano
1 teaspoon freshly ground pepper
½ teaspoon salt
2 pounds flap steaks, butterflied, ¼-inch thick
½ cup bitter orange juice or regular orange juice
2 cloves garlic, minced
½ red onion, cut into three ¼-inch-thick rounds
6 sprigs cilantro
½ teaspoon olive oil

Suggested toppings

Avocado Crema (see page 47)
Roasted Poblano Chile Strips (see page 22)
Chile de Árbol Salsa (see page 6)
Chopped onion and cilantro
Limes, cut into wedges

1. In a small bowl, combine the paprika, cumin, thyme, oregano, pepper, and salt.

2. On a large plate or baking sheet, pat the steaks dry with a paper towel, then sprinkle them with the spice blend, rubbing the spices into the meat. Put the steaks into a medium-size bowl and pour in the orange juice. Add the garlic, and mix well with your hands. Break up the onion rounds and tuck the rings and cilantro sprigs amongst the steaks. Cover and marinate at least 2 hours, preferably overnight. Stir the mixture once or twice while it is marinating.

3. Over a hot charcoal grill, or a cast-iron griddle or large pan heated for 3 minutes over high heat and coated with the olive oil, place a steak. Cook the steak for about 2 minutes, then flip and cook for 1 minute, or until medium rare.

4. On a large cutting board, cut the meat across the grain into ¼-inch strips. Then cut the strips into pieces about ½ inch long.

5. Serve immediately on warm corn or flour tortillas, topped with Avocado Crema, Roasted Poblano Chile Strips, Chile de Árbol Salsa, and chopped onion and cilantro, with lime wedges on the side.

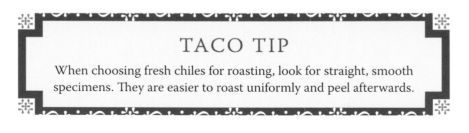

TACO TIP

When choosing fresh chiles for roasting, look for straight, smooth specimens. They are easier to roast uniformly and peel afterwards.

GRILLED CHICKEN BREAST TACO
Taco de Pollo al Carbón

Down on the border, in the town of Tecate, Baja California Norte, is a tiny taco stand called El Pollo Velóz. With a mesquite grill, they will school you with tender and juicy chicken breast tacos. Dressed with avocado crema, cilantro, and grilled jalapeños spritzed with lime, this is my tribute to the "Speedy Chicken." Look no further for perfection in a taco.

MAKES 8 TACOS

Corn or flour tortillas

Filling

2 to 3 boneless, skinless chicken breasts (about 1 pound)
1 tablespoon olive oil
Zest of 1 lemon
1 medium clove garlic, minced
Salt and freshly ground pepper

Suggested toppings

Avocado Crema (see page 47)
Chile de Árbol Salsa (see page 6)
Chopped onion and cilantro
Limes, cut into wedges

1. Lay one chicken breast flat on a cutting board. Place the palm of one hand flat on the breast to keep it from moving. With a sharp 6-inch or longer knife, slice horizontally through the breast, creating two pieces of nearly equal thickness. If the pieces are uneven or more than ½ inch thick, put them in a 1-gallon plastic bag and pound them with a meat-tenderizing mallet or the bottom of a small cast-iron pan until they are a uniform thickness. Put the breast pieces in a bowl. Repeat the process with the remaining chicken breasts.

2. In a small bowl, combine the olive oil, lemon zest, and garlic. Pour the oil mixture over the chicken pieces and swirl them around to coat all sides. Cover the bowl and put it in the refrigerator. Marinate for 2 to 6 hours.

3. On a charcoal or gas grill over medium-high heat, cook the breast pieces for 1 to 2 minutes. Flip them and cook on the other side for about 1 minute, or until cooked through. To check for doneness, cut into the thickest piece. If it is still pink, flip the chicken and cook it for an additional 1 to 2 minutes.

4. Place the chicken immediately onto a cutting board and slice the pieces into ¼-inch-wide strips. Then slice the strips into pieces about 1 inch long.

5. Serve immediately on warm corn or flour tortillas, topped with Avocado Crema, Chile de Árbol Salsa, and chopped onion and cilantro, with lime wedges on the side.

TACO TIP

To clean dust from larger dried chiles, wipe them with a slightly moistened cloth. To clean smaller chiles, such as *chiles de árbol*, place them in a colander, run water over them, and shake to remove excess water.

TACO EL PERRÓN

Taco El Perrón

Following a taco thread on an Internet forum, I learned about a killer taco place in Rosarito, Baja California, called El Yaqui. The taquería serves a legendary taco called *El Perrón*, or Big Dog, referring to its large size. When we arrived at 10:30 a.m., they were pumping out the tacos, cooking their *arrachera* (flap meat) in big strips. When it comes off the live-oak wood fire, the cooks chop the meat up and pile it into these massive tacos, which also contain cheese, pinto beans, guacamole, and two salsas. Ask your butcher to cut your flap steaks into pieces 12 to 18 inches long and about 1 to 2 inches thick.

MAKES 8 TACOS

8 flour tortillas, preferably 8-inch size

Filling

3 tablespoons paprika
½ teaspoon ground cumin
½ teaspoon dried thyme
½ teaspoon dried oregano
1 teaspoon freshly ground pepper
½ teaspoon salt
1 pound flap steak
½ cup bitter orange juice or regular orange juice
2 cloves garlic, minced
Whole Pinto Beans (see page 19)
½ teaspoon olive oil
¾ pound Oaxaca or mozzarella cheese, cut into 16 slices

Suggested toppings

Chunky Guacamole (see page 14)
Fresh Tomato Salsa (see page 2)
Chile de Árbol Salsa (see page 6)

1. In a small bowl, combine the paprika, cumin, thyme, oregano, pepper, and salt.

2. On a large plate or baking sheet, pat the steak dry with a paper towel, then sprinkle it with the spice blend, rubbing the spices into the meat. Put the steak into a medium-size bowl and pour in the orange juice. Add the garlic, and mix well with your hands. Cover and marinate, refrigerated, at least 2 hours, preferably overnight. Stir the mixture once or twice while it is marinating.

3. Shortly before grilling the meat, warm the Whole Pinto Beans in a pot.

4. Over a hot charcoal grill, or a cast-iron griddle or large pan heated for 5 minutes over medium-high heat and coated with the olive oil, cook the steak until medium rare, flipping every 2 minutes, about 8 minutes total.

5. On a large cutting board, cut the meat across the grain into ¼-inch strips. Then cut the strips into pieces about ½ inch long.

6. While the meat is cooking, heat the tortillas on a griddle or in a large cast-iron pan over medium heat. Melt 2 slices of cheese on one side of each tortilla. Place the tortillas on plates, topped with some of the cooked steak, Whole Pinto Beans, Chunky Guacamole, Fresh Tomato Salsa, and Chile de Árbol Salsa.

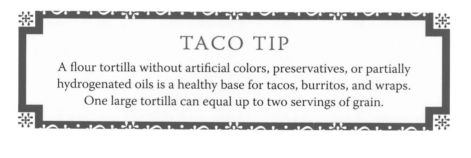

TACO TIP

A flour tortilla without artificial colors, preservatives, or partially hydrogenated oils is a healthy base for tacos, burritos, and wraps. One large tortilla can equal up to two servings of grain.

BAJA FISH TACO
Taco de Pescado

The principles of perfect breaded fish tacos are clean oil; quality fish; thin, crisp, and tasty breading; and killer condiments. The tacos must also be served hot from the fryer—no sitting around. I prefer to serve the fish on top of the Mexican Crema and shredded cabbage for a novel presentation. Use a firm white fish such as halibut, orange roughy, or tilapia that will hold together during the breading and frying. Though not officially a taco dorado, fish taco frying techniques are similar enough to be placed in the same category.

MAKES 16 TACOS

 Corn tortillas

Filling

 1 cup flour
 ¼ teaspoon baking powder
 ¼ teaspoon dried oregano
 ½ teaspoon salt
 ¼ teaspoon freshly ground pepper
 ½ teaspoon powdered mustard
 ½ cup plus 2 tablespoons water
 ½ cup beer
 Vegetable oil, enough to fill pan to 1 inch deep
 2 pounds raw firm white fish fillets, cut into 1-inch-wide strips

Suggested toppings

 Mexican Crema (see page 10)
 Finely grated green cabbage
 Avocado Crema (see page 47)
 Fresh Tomato Salsa (see page 2)
 Chile de Árbol Salsa (see page 6)
 Chopped onion and cilantro
 Limes, cut into wedges

1. In a small bowl, whisk the flour, baking powder, oregano, salt, pepper, and powdered mustard until combined. In a medium-size bowl, combine

the water and beer, then gradually whisk in the dry ingredients until just incorporated. Don't overmix.

2. In a medium-size cast-iron skillet or other heavy pan, fill with oil to 1 inch deep and heat the oil to 350°F. The surface of the oil will glisten. If it smokes, turn the heat down a little.

3. Holding the fish strips by one end, dip them into the batter, coating lightly, then gently set them into the oil. If they brown in less than a minute, turn the heat down a little. Gently flip the pieces over when golden, about 1 to 2 minutes, and cook for an additional 1 to 2 minutes. Remove the fish from the oil with a slotted spoon and let drain on a paper towel–lined plate.

4. Serve on warm tortillas, topped with Mexican Crema; cabbage; your choice of Avocado Crema, Fresh Tomato Salsa, Chile de Árbol Salsa; and chopped onion and cilantro, with lime wedges on the side.

TACO TIP

Corn tortillas are low in fat and sodium. They are also a great gluten-free alternative to bread.

SHRIMP AND SOFRITO TACO

Taco de Camarones en Sofrito

These tacos are cooked in a pan, or *sarten*. Use a good one because because these tacos deserve the best. Many Latin American dishes are built on *sofrito*, a sautéed mixture of onion, bell pepper, and tomato. These shrimp tacos are elegant, pairing a classic sofrito with a splash of tequila and lime. A nice twist during assembly is to put the Mexican Crema and cabbage under the shrimp for a flawless appearance.

Note: *To peel the tomato, put it in a small pot of boiling water until the skin splits, about 2 minutes. Immediately place it in cold water to stop the cooking, and then peel.*

MAKES 12 TACOS

    Corn tortillas

Filling

    5 tablespoons olive oil, divided
    ½ medium white onion, finely chopped
    ½ medium red bell pepper, finely chopped
    1 medium tomato, peeled, seeded, and finely chopped
    1 tablespoon butter
    6 cloves garlic, finely chopped
    1¼ pounds medium shrimp (about 48), peeled and deveined
    ¼ cup tequila
    2 tablespoons finely chopped cilantro

Suggested toppings

    Mexican Crema (see page 10)
    Finely grated cabbage
    Thinly sliced avocado
    Fresh Tomato Salsa (see page 2)
    Chile de Árbol Salsa (see page 6)
    Limes, cut into wedges

1. For the sofrito, in a medium-size pan over medium heat, heat 3 tablespoons of the olive oil. Add the onion and sauté, stirring occasionally, until

lightly brown, about 10 minutes. Add the red pepper and cook, stirring occasionally, for an additional 7 minutes. Add the tomato and cook, stirring, until the liquid has nearly evaporated, 5 minutes or less. Pour the sofrito into a small bowl and set aside.

2. For the shrimp, in a medium-size pan over medium heat, heat the remaining olive oil, the butter, and half the garlic. Cook, stirring, for 3 minutes. Add the shrimp and the rest of the garlic. Cook for an additional 3 minutes. Raise the heat to medium-high, add the sofrito and tequila, and cook, stirring, for 4 minutes, or until most of the liquid has evaporated. Remove from the heat and stir in the cilantro.

3. Serve on warm tortillas, topped with Mexican Crema, cabbage, avocado slices, Fresh Tomato Salsa, and Chile de Árbol Salsa, with lime wedges on the side.

TACO TIP

Serve chopped white onions and cilantro in separate bowls so that diners can customize their own tacos.

SPICED GROUND TURKEY TACO
Taco de Picadillo de Guajolote

Turkey doesn't get much press, unless it's Thanksgiving in the United States, or it's uttered in the same breath with *mole poblano*, the famous chile-chocolate sauce, in Mexico. Here it pairs nicely with smoky, sweet Seven Chile Salsa and crumbled Cotija. For a neat presentation, I like to spread some Seven Chile Salsa on the warm tortilla before laying down the turkey (see picture on page 28).

MAKES 8 TO 12 TACOS

Corn or flour tortillas

Filling
1 teaspoon coriander seeds
¼ teaspoon cumin seeds
1 tablespoons olive oil
2 tablespoons finely chopped white onion
1 clove garlic, finely chopped
1 large tomato, finely chopped
1 pound ground turkey
2 tablespoons paprika
¼ teaspoon freshly ground pepper
¼ teaspoon dried thyme
1 teaspoon salt

Suggested toppings
Seven Chile Salsa (see page 9)
¼ pound Cotija cheese, crumbled
Chopped onion and cilantro
Limes, cut into wedges

1. In a small cast-iron or other heavy pan over medium heat, lightly toast the coriander and cumin seeds, shaking them constantly, for about 3 minutes. Let cool and grind with a spice grinder or mortar and pestle.

2. In a medium-size pan over medium heat, heat the olive oil. Add the onion and garlic and sauté for 3 minutes. Add the tomato and sauté until most of the liquid has evaporated, about 4 to 5 minutes.

3. Meanwhile, put the ground turkey in a medium-size bowl and add the reserved ground coriander and cumin, the paprika, pepper, thyme, and salt. Mix well. Raise the heat to medium-high and add the turkey to the tomato mixture in the pan, stirring to incorporate, and cook until the turkey is cooked through, about 12 minutes.

4. Serve on warm corn or flour tortillas, topped with Seven Chile Salsa, crumbled Cotija cheese, and chopped onion and cilantro, with lime wedges on the side.

TACO TIP

Grilled green onions are delicious with any type of taco.
Coat them lightly with oil and sprinkle with salt. Cook over medium heat in a heavy pan or grill them on the coolest part of the grill. Serve warm with tacos.

GARLIC—WILD MUSHROOM TACO WITH CREAMED CORN AND MORITA SALSA

Taco de Hongos Silvestres con Salsa de Elote y Morita

I live in the mountains, and here, autumn is wild mushroom heaven. Many parts of Mexico are also thick with mushrooms after the first autumn rains. This recipe is summer meets fall, with the last sweet corn and the first tender mushrooms joining on a warm tortilla.

MAKES 8 TACOS

> Corn or flour tortillas

Filling

> 2 dried *morita* or chipotle chiles, or 2 canned chipotle chiles, removed
>   from the sauce
> 3 ears of sweet corn, shucked
> 3 tablespoons olive oil, divided
> ½ medium white onion, finely chopped
> 1 cup vegetable broth
> Salt
> Freshly ground pepper
> 2 tablespoons butter
> 2 cloves garlic, minced
> 1 pound wild mushrooms

Suggested toppings

> ¼ pound *queso fresco*, crumbled
> Chopped cilantro

1. For the sauce, stem and seed the moritas, then put them in a small bowl and cover them with boiling water. Cover and let sit until softened, about 30 minutes. Remove with a slotted spoon and set aside.

2. Heat a *comal* or large cast-iron pan on medium for a few minutes, then roast the ears of corn, turning frequently, until lightly browned, about 5 to 7

minutes per ear. Let them cool, then cut the corn off the cob and put it into a food processor or blender.

3. Meanwhile, in a small pan over medium heat, add 1 tablespoon of the olive oil and sauté the onions until translucent, about 5 to 7 minutes. Add them to the food processor and return the pan to the stove. Add the reserved chiles and half of the vegetable broth to the blender and blend until smooth. Continue adding vegetable broth until the blend is easily pourable. Add salt and pepper to taste. Return the sauce to the pan and cook over medium heat, stirring, for 10 minutes.

4. For the mushrooms, in a large pan, heat the remaining olive oil and the butter over medium heat. Add half of the garlic and sauté for 1 minute. Add the mushrooms and the second half of the garlic, and cook, stirring occasionally, until the mushrooms have released their juices and the liquid has evaporated, about 10 minutes. The mushrooms will still be slightly firm when done.

5. Serve on warm corn or flour tortillas, topped with the corn sauce, crumbled queso fresco, and cilantro.

TACO TIP

When grilling meats, try to get mesquite charcoal for a great flavor. Also try soaking wood chips and placing them on the coals for a smokier taste.

ZUCCHINI AND CHEESE
TACO DORADO

Taco Dorado de Calabacita y Queso

At the height of summer, I'm constantly looking for new ways to lure the family into eating more zucchini. Enter *tacos dorados*. Also known as rolled tacos or *taquitos*, they are temptation personified (or is that *tacofied*?). With "zukes" and melted cheese inside a crispy, fried shell, these, or any golden tacos, are likely to be devoured as fast as you can make them.

MAKES 12 TACOS

12 corn tortillas

Filling

¼ cup plus ¼ teaspoon olive oil
3 small zucchinis (about 1½ pounds), cut into ¼-inch cubes
1 cup Quick Tomato Salsa (see page 4)
¼ teaspoon dried oregano
¼ teaspoon dried thyme
½ teaspoon salt
Freshly ground pepper
¾ pound Oaxaca or mozzarella cheese, grated
Lard or vegetable oil, enough to fill pan to ½ inch deep

Suggested toppings

Mexican Crema (see page 10)
Chile de Árbol Salsa (see page 6)
Fresh Tomatillo Salsa (see page 10)
Shredded lettuce (optional)

1. In a medium-size pan, heat ¼ cup of the olive oil over medium heat. Add the zucchini and cook, stirring occasionally, until it begins to soften, about 5 to 7 minutes. Add the Quick Tomato Salsa, oregano, thyme, salt, and pepper to taste, and cook, stirring, until the liquid has evaporated and sauce has thickened, about 10 minutes. Remove from heat and let cool.

2. In a medium-size pan over medium heat, add the ¼ teaspoon olive oil. Put in two tortillas, flipping them over and sliding them around in the pan to coat lightly with the oil and warm them, about 1 minute. Stack the tortillas on a plate. Repeat the process with the remaining tortillas, adding a bit more oil if needed.

3. Using a slotted spoon, put about 3 to 4 tablespoons of the zucchini mixture at one edge of a tortilla. Sprinkle about 1 tablespoon of the Oaxaca cheese on top of the zucchini. Fold the edge of the tortilla over the mixture and roll tightly. Carefully place the taco on a plate, seam side down to keep it from unrolling. Repeat with the remaining tortillas.

4. For frying the tacos, in a medium-size cast-iron or other heavy pan over medium heat, melt enough lard or add enough oil to fill pan to ½ inch deep. Heat the lard to 350°F. The surface of the oil will glisten. If it smokes, turn the heat down a little. Place the tacos in the pan seam side up, and fry until golden, about 1 minute. Using tongs, roll the tacos over and cook the other side until golden, about 1 minute longer. Remove the tacos and place them on a paper towel–lined plate to drain.

5. Serve immediately with Mexican Crema, Chile de Árbol Salsa, Fresh Tomatillo Salsa, and shredded lettuce.

CHORIZO AND CACTUS
TACO DORADO
Taco Dorado de Chorizo y Nopales

Two fantastic ingredients combine here to make a stellar and somewhat novel taco. Fresh *nopales*, or cactus paddles, are available in Mexican markets. Ask to be sure the spines have been removed! They're also available in jars.

MAKES 18 TACOS

18 corn tortillas

Filling

1¼ teaspoons olive oil, divided
1 pound chorizo, casing removed, broken into small pieces
4 tablespoons salt
3 fresh nopales (or 1 jar nopales, drained), cut into ¼- by 2-inch strips
Lard or vegetable oil, enough to fill pan to ½ inch deep

Suggested toppings

Mexican Crema (see page 10)
Fresh Tomato Salsa (see page 2)
Fresh Tomatillo Salsa (see page 10)
Shredded lettuce (optional)

1. In a medium-size cast-iron or other heavy pan over medium heat, add 1 teaspoon of the oil and tilt pan to coat. Add the chorizo and cook, stirring occasionally, until cooked through, about 7 minutes. Using a slotted spoon, remove the chorizo to a medium-size bowl.

2. In a large pot, bring 4 quarts of water to a boil. Add the salt and nopales and boil for 15 to 20 minutes. Drain in a colander, rinsing under cold water for 5 minutes, until the slippery coating is washed off. Drain the nopales well and add them to the bowl with the chorizo. Stir well.

3. In a medium-size pan over medium heat, add the remaining olive oil. Put in two tortillas, flipping them over and sliding them around in the pan to coat lightly with the oil and warm them, about 1 minute. Stack the tortillas on a

plate. Repeat the process with the remaining tortillas, adding a bit more oil if needed.

4. Put about 3 to 4 tablespoons of the nopales/chorizo mixture at one edge of a tortilla. Fold the edge over the mixture and roll tightly. Carefully place the taco on a plate, seam side down to keep it from unrolling. Repeat with the remaining tortillas.

5. For frying the tacos, in a medium-size cast-iron or other heavy pan over medium heat, melt enough lard or add enough oil to fill ½ inch deep. Heat the lard to 350°F. The surface of the oil will glisten. If it smokes, turn the heat down a little. Place the tacos in the pan seam side up, and fry until golden, about 1 minute. Using tongs, roll the tacos over and cook the other side until golden, about 1 minute longer. Remove the tacos and place them on a paper towel–lined plate to drain.

6. Serve immediately with Mexican Crema, Fresh Tomato Salsa, and shredded lettuce.

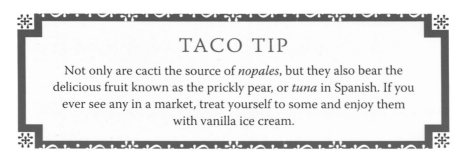

TACO TIP

Not only are cacti the source of *nopales*, but they also bear the delicious fruit known as the prickly pear, or *tuna* in Spanish. If you ever see any in a market, treat yourself to some and enjoy them with vanilla ice cream.

FISH AND SOFRITO
TACO DORADO

Taco Dorado de Pescado con Sofrito

Sofrito is the basis of many Spanish and Latin American dishes. The long sautéing of the onions brings out their sweetness. Here I include Anaheim chiles, tomato, and cilantro for a tasty and slightly spicy mixture to go with the fish.

Note: *To peel the tomato, put it in a small pot of boiling water until the skin splits, about 2 minutes. Immediately place it in cold water to stop the cooking, and then peel.*

MAKES 12 TACOS

    12 corn tortillas

Filling

    1 tablespoon plus ½ teaspoon olive oil, divided
    ¼ medium white onion, finely chopped
    1 clove garlic, finely chopped
    2 red Anaheim chiles, finely chopped (substitute green if red are
      unavailable)
    1 medium tomato, peeled, seeded, and finely chopped
    1 tablespoon finely chopped cilantro
    4 tilapia fillets (about 1 pound)
    Lard or vegetable oil, enough to fill pan to ½ inch deep

Suggested toppings

    Mexican Crema (see page 10)
    Avocado and Jalapeño Salsa (see page 15)
    Chile de Árbol Salsa (see page 6)
    Fresh Tomatillo Salsa (see page 10)
    Shredded lettuce, preferably romaine
    Limes, cut into wedges

1. For the sofrito, in a medium-size pan over medium heat, heat 1 tablespoon of the olive oil. Add the onion and garlic and sauté, stirring occasionally, until lightly brown, about 10 minutes. Add the Anaheims and cook, stirring

occasionally, for an additional 7 minutes. Add the tomato and cook, stirring, until the liquid has nearly evaporated, 5 minutes. Pour the sofrito into a medium-size bowl; add the cilantro and mix well. Set aside. Return the pan to the heat.

2. Add ¼ teaspoon of the olive oil, swirl to coat the bottom of the pan, and put in the fillets. Cook for about 3 minutes per side, or until cooked through. Add the fillets to the bowl with the sofrito and break them up with a fork, stirring to incorporate.

3. In a medium-size pan over medium heat, add the remaining olive oil. Put in two tortillas, flipping them over and sliding them around in the pan to coat lightly with the oil and warm them, about 1 minute. Stack the tortillas on a plate. Repeat the process with the remaining tortillas, adding a bit more oil if needed.

4. Using a slotted spoon, put about 3 to 4 tablespoons of the fish mixture at one edge of a tortilla. Fold the edge over the mixture and roll tightly. Carefully place the taco on a plate, seam side down to keep it from unrolling. Repeat with the remaining tortillas.

5. For frying the tacos, in a medium-size cast-iron or other heavy pan over medium heat, melt enough lard or add enough oil to fill pan to ½ inch deep. Heat the lard to 350°F. The surface of the oil will glisten. If it smokes, turn the heat down a little. Place the tacos in the pan seam side up, and fry until golden, about 1 minute. Using tongs, roll the tacos over and cook the other side until golden, about 1 minute longer. Remove the tacos and place them on a paper towel–lined plate to drain.

6. Serve immediately with Mexican Crema, Avocado and Jalapeño Salsa, Chile de Árbol Salsa, Fresh Tomatillo Salsa, and shredded lettuce, with lime wedges on the side.

DRINKS AND DESSERTS

Horchata
Tamarind Agua Fresca
Spicy Cherry Agua Fresca
Michelada
Ryan's Blackberry Margarita
Fruit Granitas
Blackberry Corn Drink
Café de Olla
Spicy Hot Fudge Tacos

HORCHATA
Horchata

If you've never tried *horchata*, please do. It has a nourishing and refreshing substance, unlike anything made from rice that you've ever tried. It's a triumph of the imagination: old world grain meets new world minds. For a festive touch, serve from a widemouthed gallon jar with a ladle.

MAKES ABOUT 4 QUARTS

    1 cup rice
    1 pound blanched almonds
    2-inch cinnamon stick
    4 quarts water
    2½ cups sugar

1. Grind the rice in a spice grinder or blender. Put the ground rice, almonds, and cinnamon stick in a large bowl. Heat 7 cups of the water to about 140°F and pour over the ingredients, stirring to incorporate. Cover and let sit overnight.

2. Put half of the rice mixture in a blender and blend until smooth, about 2 minutes. Add 2½ cups of the water and blend just to incorporate, about 30 seconds. Set a sieve lined with 2 or 3 layers of cheesecloth over a large bowl and pour in the mixture. Using a spatula or the back of a spoon, press and stir the mixture to strain out the liquid. Then twist the ends of the cheesecloth and squeeze the rice ball to expel the remaining liquid. Repeat the process with the other half of the rice mixture and 2½ cups of the water.

3. Add the remaining 4 cups water and slowly stir in the sugar, adding just enough to suit your liking. Pour into a 1-gallon jar and refrigerate. Stir well before serving. The horchata will keep in the refrigerator for a week.

TAMARIND AGUA FRESCA
Agua Fresca de Tamarindo

Just picturing the tart, pasty tamarind pod in my head makes my mouth pucker. This classic *agua fresca* is perky and tropical, certain to quench your thirst on a hot summer day.

MAKES ABOUT 4 QUARTS

> 4 quarts water
> 2 pounds tamarind paste
> 2 cups sugar

1. In a medium-size pot, bring the water, tamarind paste, and sugar to a boil for 1 minute. Cover, cool and let sit for 1 hour.

2. Working in batches, transfer the mixture to a blender and pulse a few times. Set a sieve over a large bowl and pour in the mixture. Using a spatula or the back of a spoon, press and stir the mixture to strain out the liquid. Pour into a 1-gallon jar and refrigerate. Stir well before serving. The agua fresca will keep in the refrigerator for a week.

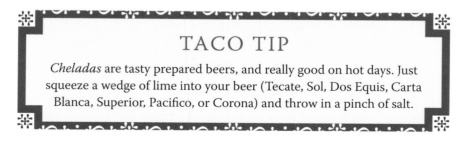

TACO TIP

Cheladas are tasty prepared beers, and really good on hot days. Just squeeze a wedge of lime into your beer (Tecate, Sol, Dos Equis, Carta Blanca, Superior, Pacifico, or Corona) and throw in a pinch of salt.

SPICY CHERRY AGUA FRESCA
Agua Fresca Picosa de Cereza

This slightly fiery *agua fresca* will keep you alert while you eat your tacos. From Nikki R. Cohen of The Hungry Cat restaurants in Hollywood and Santa Barbara, California, it dances intriguingly between tangy sweetness and invigorating spiciness. If Pancho Villa had been born a hundred years later, he'd be cooling his chops with this baby.

MAKES ABOUT 4 QUARTS

> 11½ cups water, divided
> 2½ cups sugar, plus more for coating chiles
> 4 to 5 Fresno chiles, stems and seeds intact, cut into 6 strips each
> 3 to 4 pounds Bing cherries, pitted
> Juice of 8 lemons (approximately 1½ cups)

1. First, make a Fresno simple syrup by bringing 2½ cups of the water, the sugar, and the Fresno strips to a boil in a medium-size saucepan. Simmer for 15 minutes and remove from heat.

2. With a slotted spoon, transfer the Fresno strips to an oven rack and let them dry. Let the syrup cool, then strain it through a fine mesh sieve and set it aside. When the Fresno strips are dry, dip them in sugar, lay them on a plate, and set aside.

3. In a juicer, juice the cherries to get 3 cups of juice. Alternatively, put the cherries in a blender with some of the water and blend.

4. Set a sieve over a large bowl and pour in the cherry mixture. Using a spatula or the back of a spoon, press and stir the mixture to strain out the liquid. Add the remaining water, the lemon juice, and the Fresno simple syrup to taste. Pour into a 1-gallon glass jar and refrigerate. Stir well before serving. Serve over ice and garnish with some of the reserved candied Fresno strips. The agua fresca will keep in the refrigerator for a week.

MICHELADA
Michelada

Mi chelada means "my chelada" in Spanish. Yes, it is—yours to make and drink while relaxing in the shade on a hot day. Maggi, a popular brand of sauce in Mexico, is available at Latin American and Chinese markets and online. Look for the little bottles of liquid sauce, not the Maggi bouillon products.

MAKES 1 MICHELADA

> Coarse salt
> Lime wedge
> Juice of ½ lime (approximately 1 tablespoon)
> 2 dashes Worcestershire sauce
> 1 dash Tabasco, or other hot sauce such as Tapatío or Huichol
> 1 pinch freshly ground pepper
> 1 dash Maggi Seasoning Sauce
> 1 dash soy sauce (optional)
> One 12-ounce bottle Mexican beer

Cover the surface of a small plate or bowl with salt. Rub the rim of a tall glass with a lime wedge and press the rim into the salt to coat. Fill the glass with ice and add the lime juice, Worcestershire, Tabasco, pepper, Maggi, and soy sauce, if using. Stir with a long spoon. Pour in the beer and stir again. Garnish with the lime wedge.

RYAN'S BLACKBERRY MARGARITA

Margarita de Moras de Ryan

In the heat of summer, with an abundance of sweet, fresh blackberries everywhere, this margarita shines. In fact, it's one of master mixologist Ryan Magarian's "go-to summer-thyme refreshers" at backyard dinner parties (or a *taquiza*, perhaps!). Here, the technique called muddling, which is the bruising of herbs and the light crushing of fruit, releases the essential oils contained in the thyme and mixes it with the blackberries. Cheers to Ryan for sharing his recipe.

Note: *A muddler is essentially a wooden handle used to crush herbs and spices directly in a cocktail shaker or glass. It can be found in houseware stores. A decent substitute is any household utensil that has a wooden handle with a blunt end. Use a muddler much like a pestle, smashing the ingredients to release their essences.*

MAKES 2 COCKTAILS

Simple Syrup
>   2 cups water
>   2 cups granulated sugar

Margarita
>   1 teaspoon vodka
>   2 to 3 limes (to make 1½ ounces lime juice)
>   14 fresh blackberries
>   2 sprigs fresh thyme, plus 2 sprigs for garnish
>   ½ ounce Cointreau
>   3 ounces El Tesoro Platinum tequila
>   Ice (about 6 to 8 cubes home freezer size)
>   2 ounces brut champagne

1. To make the simple syrup, combine the water and sugar in a saucepan and heat over medium heat until sugar is dissolved. Allow to cool, then add the teaspoon vodka as a preservative. Refrigerate until ready to use.

2. Using a citrus juicer or lime expresser, juice the limes and set aside.

3. In a shaker or jar, add the blackberries and two sprigs of thyme and muddle until the berries are fairly well crushed, about 8 to 10 presses with the flat side of the muddler.

4. Add the Cointreau, tequila, lime juice, and 1½ ounces simple syrup to the muddled mixture.

5. Add several pieces of ice to the shaker or jar, leaving some room at the top. Then place the lid on the shaker and shake vigorously for 6 seconds. Remove lid and strain contents into two chilled cocktail glasses.

6. Top each margarita with 1 ounce brut champagne, then lay a sprig of thyme across the top and serve.

FRUIT GRANITAS
Agua Fresca Helada

This recipe is tasty, refreshing, and very easy. Simply make any of the *aguas frescas* (see pages 85 and 86) and follow these directions.

MAKES 8 CUPS

   2 quarts agua fresca, any variety

1. Pour the agua fresca into a 9- by 13-inch baking dish, or another dish that is wide and shallow. Put the dish in the freezer.

2. About once an hour, remove the dish from the freezer and stir with a spoon, breaking up the ice that forms along the edge of the dish with the edge of the spoon. This will give the drink a nice, grainy texture. Allow 4 to 6 hours for the entire process.

3. When the agua fresca is completely frozen into grainy ice, scoop it into individual ice cream cups and return them to the freezer until ready to serve.

BLACKBERRY CORN DRINK

Atole de Moras

I love *atole*, the ancient Mesoamerican corn-based drink, and I love blackberries, which grow in profusion around my Pacific Northwest home. This is an ideal warm dessert after a cool-weather taco meal—tasty and nutritious. It's also a great drink to start the day. Kids love to dip cinnamon sticks in the atole and slurp it off. Atole's base ingredient, a special cornmeal-like flour called *masa harina*, is available at Latin American markets, many supermarkets, and online.

Note: *To break up cones of* piloncillo, *the Mexican brown sugar, use the thick edge of a cleaver or a hammer.*

MAKES ABOUT 5 CUPS

> 5 cups blackberries, fresh or frozen
> 2½ cups water
> 3 tablespoons piloncillo or dark brown sugar
> ⅓ cup masa harina
> 2-inch cinnamon sticks, for garnish

1. In a medium-size pot over medium-low heat, combine the blackberries and water and cook, covered, for about 10 minutes, or until the berries are very soft, stirring occasionally. Remove from heat, let cool, and transfer to a food processor or blender. Blend until smooth, about 1 minute. Set a sieve over a medium-size bowl and pour in the blackberry purée. Using a spatula or the back of a spoon, press and stir the mixture to strain out as much liquid as possible.

2. Return the strained mixture to the pot, add the piloncillo, and warm over low heat until the piloncillo is dissolved. Whisk in the masa and cook over low heat, stirring frequently, for about 10 minutes, until the atole has thickened to a gravylike consistency. If the mixture seems too thick, add a little water. Serve hot in mugs garnished with a cinnamon stick.

CAFÉ DE OLLA
Café de Olla

Traditionally made in a *cazuela*, or earthenware pot, and served in earthenware mugs, Café de Olla, a Mexican-style coffee, is brewed with cinnamon and served with *piloncillo*, Mexican brown sugar. It's a satisfying way to end a meal. ***Note:*** *To break up piloncillo cones, use the thick edge of a cleaver or a hammer.*

MAKES ABOUT 4 CUPS

> 5 cups water
> ¾ to 1 cup coarsely ground medium-dark roast coffee
> 2-inch cinnamon stick
> 6 ounces piloncillo, broken into small pieces, for serving

Put the water in a medium-size pot and bring to a boil. Add the coffee and cinnamon and bring to a boil again. Turn off the heat, cover the pot, and let steep for 5 minutes. Set a sieve over a serving pot and pour in the mixture. Serve with the piloncillo pieces on the side.

TACO TIP

Consider buying fair trade Mexican coffee for your Café de Olla. Some sources include www.equalexchange.coop, www.peacecoffee.com, deansbeans.com, and cafecampesino.com.

SPICY HOT FUDGE TACOS
Taco de Salsa Picante de Chocolate

The Aztecs drank *xocolatl*, an elixir made of freshly ground cacao beans and hot chiles. A nod to xocolatl, this fudge sauce is a bit spicy, with just a touch of cayenne and ancho chile powder. Pour it over crepes and vanilla ice cream and you have a dessert taco like no other. Don't let the long recipe scare you— all the steps are simple. This recipe makes about 2 cups of hot fudge sauce. Leftover sauce can be refrigerated for up to two weeks and drizzled on ice cream, blended into milkshakes, or stirred into hot coffee for an interesting mocha.

MAKES 5 SERVINGS

Crepe Tortillas

    2 eggs
    ¾ cup milk
    ¼ cup water
    ¾ pastry or all-purpose flour
    ¼ cup fine corn flour
    ⅜ teaspoon salt
    4 tablespoons unsalted butter, melted

Spicy Hot Fudge Sauce

    10 ounces semisweet chocolate (at least 70 percent cacao content)
    ⅓ cup Dutch cocoa powder
    ¼ teaspoon cayenne
    ½ teaspoon ancho chile powder
    ¾ cup light corn syrup
    ⅓ cup sugar
    ⅓ cup heavy cream
    ⅓ cup water
    Pinch of salt
    3 tablespoons unsalted butter, cut into ¼-inch pieces
    1 teaspoon vanilla extract

    ½ gallon vanilla ice cream
    ¼ cup toasted almonds, finely chopped

1. For the Crepe Tortillas, put the egg, milk, and water in a food processor or blender, and blend until smooth, about 5 seconds. Add the pastry flour, corn flour, and salt, and blend for 5 more seconds. With a spatula, scrape down the sides of the container, and blend for 5 more seconds. Pour the batter into a medium-size bowl, cover, and put in the refrigerator to rest, at least 2 hours, but ideally overnight.

2. Over medium heat, warm a 7-inch crepe pan or other seasoned pan with sloped sides. When the pan is hot, brush the surface with a little of the butter. Add 3 tablespoons of the batter to the pan and tilt the pan so that the batter coats the entire bottom. (If the batter is too thick to pour and spread out in the pan quickly, add a little water or milk to it in the bowl while whisking. If the crepe sets before it covers the pan, discard the crepe—or finish cooking and eat it—lower the heat slightly, and wave the pan in the air for about 15 seconds to cool it off. Begin a new crepe.) Cook until the edges of the crepe begin to dry and pull away from the pan, about 1 minute. Slide a spatula or knife under the edge to loosen the crepe and flip it over, cooking the second side just until set, about 30 seconds. Transfer to a plate.

3. Repeat with the rest of the crepe batter, adding additional butter to the pan as needed, until you have used all of the batter. You should have 9 or 10 crepes. When the crepes are all cooked, cover them and refrigerate until ready to use.

4. For the Spicy Hot Fudge Sauce, in a double boiler, melt the chocolate, whisking often, until smooth, about 3 to 5 minutes. Alternatively, melt the chocolate in a medium-size glass bowl in the microwave on high, stirring every 1 minute. Once the chocolate is melted, whisk in the cocoa powder, cayenne, and ancho powder until dissolved.

5. In a medium-size saucepan, simmer the corn syrup, sugar, cream, water, and salt over medium heat, stirring frequently, until thickened, about 4 minutes.

6. Remove the saucepan from the stove and whisk in the butter and vanilla. Let the mixture cool for 2 minutes, then whisk in the melted chocolate mixture until smooth, about 1 minute.

7. To assemble, work quickly so the ice cream doesn't melt. Place a cold crepe on a cold plate. With a small ice cream scoop or a spoon, put 3 to 4 scoops of vanilla ice cream near the edge of the crepe closest to you. Flip the edge of the crepe over the ice cream and roll it up. Place the rolled crepe, seam-side down, on the plate. Repeat with the remaining crepes. For each serving, include 2 rolled crepes. Pour 2 to 3 tablespoons of warmed Spicy Hot Fudge Sauce over the crepes, sprinkle with the toasted almonds, and serve.

REFERENCES AND RESOURCES

SELECTED BIBLIOGRAPHY

Alters Jamison, Cheryl, and Bill Jamison. *The Rancho de Chimayó Cookbook: The Traditional Cooking of New Mexico*. The Harvard Common Press: Boston, 1991.

Ávila Hernández, Dolores, et al. *Atlas cultural de mexico: Gastronomía*. Grupo Editorial Planeta: Mexico, 1988.

Bayless, Rick. *Authentic Mexican: Regional Cooking from the Heart of Mexico*. William Morrow and Company, New York, 1987.

Brennan, Kira, Ed. *Secrets of Salsa: A Bilingual Cookbook by the Mexican Women of Anderson Valley*. Chelsea Green Publishing: Vermont, 2001.

Castelló Yturbide. Teresa. *Presencia de la comida prehispanica*. Banamex: Mexico City, 1987.

Christenson, Allen J. *Popol Vuh: The Sacred Book of the Maya*. University of Oklahoma Press, 2007

DeWitt, Dave and Chuck Evans. *The Hot Sauce Bible*. The Crossing Press: California, 1996.

Facciola, Stephen. *Cornucopia: A Source Book of Edible Plants*. Kampong Publications: California, 1998.

Gironella De'Angeli, Alicia and Jorge De'Angeli. *Epazote y molcajete: Productos y técnicas de la cocina mexicana*. Larousse: Mexico City, 1993.

Kennedy, Diana. *The Cuisines of Mexico*. Harper and Row: New York, 1972.

———. *The Art of Mexican Cooking: Traditional Mexican Cooking for Aficionados*. Bantam Books: New York, 1989.

———. *From My Mexican Kitchen: Techniques and Ingredients*. Clarkson Potter: New York, 2003.

Madison, Deborah. *Vegetarian Cooking for Everyone*. Broadway Books: New York, 1997.

Martínez, Zarela. *The Food and Life of Oaxaca: Traditional Recipes from Mexico's Heart*. Macmillan: New York, 1997.

Midgley, John. *The Goodness of Peppers*. Random House: New York, 1993.

Naj, Amal. *Peppers: A Story of Hot Pursuits*. Vintage Books: New York, 1992.

Quintana, Patricia. *Puebla: La cocina de Los Angeles*. Promotores Voluntarios Del Hospital Para El Niño Poblano: Mexico City, 1992.

Szwarc, Sandy. *Real New Mexico Chile: An Insider's Guide to Cooking with Chile*. Golden West Publishers: Arizona, 1996.

FURTHER READING

American Public Media, *Marketplace*. Latino markets growing in the U.S. August 26, 2008. http://marketplace.publicradio.org/display/web/2008/08/26/el_super.

Andrews, Colman. Carolina Cocina: A wave of Mexican immigration is changing the definition of Southern cooking. *Gourmet*, September 2007.

Baños, Tomás. Asisten cinco mil comensales a Feria Nacional del Taco de Canasta. *El Sol de Tlaxcala*, December 4, 2007. http://www.oem.com.mx/elsoldetlaxcala/notas/n512540.htm.

Corona Páez, Sergio Antonio. Esas medias hermanas mexicanas llamadas "tortillas." February

2008. http://www.historiacocina.com/paises/articulos/mexico/tortillas.htm.

Dorf, John. Jesus at the taco stand. http://www.jondorf.com/jesusexcerpt.html.

Fitch, Roxana, Jergas de Habla Hispana http://www.jergasdehablahispana.org.

Henderson, Bobby. Fine Art Taco Photography. http://henderob.com

Sharpe, Patricia, The School That Salsa Built. *Gourmet*, September 2007.

Smith, Andrew F. "Tacos, Enchiladas and Refried Beans: The Invention of Mexican-American Cookery," presented at the Symposium at Oregon State University, 1999. http://food.oregonstate.edu/ref/culture/mexico_smith.html.

Tortilla Industry Association. New study finds tortillas are the second most popular bread type in America. http://www.tortilla-info.com/media_room/press/prrevenue03.htm.

——. Tortilla talk: nutritional information. http://www.tortilla-info.com/consumers/tortilla_talk/tortilla_talk.htm#facts.

Tragón, Javón, 37 taquerías que debes conocer. August 26, 2008, Chilango.com. http://www.chilango.com/restaurantes/especiales/37-taquerias-que-debes-conocer.

Mother Jones, A year without a Mexican. July/August 2000. http://www.motherjones.com/news/feature/2000/07/diaspora.html.

St. Theresa Catholic Church. Early bird tacos. http://www.sttaustin.org/index.cfm?load=page&page=159.

SOURCES FOR COOKWARE AND INGREDIENTS

Frontera Foods
www.fronterakitchens.com/shopping
(800) 509-4441, ext 120
info@fronterafoods.com
Frontera Foods is Mexican cookbook author and TV show host Rick Bayless's store.

Mesa Mexican Foods
www.mesamexicanfoods.com
P.O. Box 40663
Mesa, AZ 85274-0663
webmaster@mesamexicanfoods.com
They have a nice selection of ingredients, including dried chipotle and *morita* chiles.

MexGrocer.com
www.mexgrocer.com
4060 Morena Blvd., Suite C
San Diego, CA 92117
(877) 463-9476
info@mexgrocer.com
They carry a vast selection of ingredients and cookware, including lead-free ceramic cookware, stone *molcajetes*, a cactus knife set, and Mexican dishes. They also have dried epazote.

TortillaCocina
www.tortillacocina.com
P.O. Box 16113
Chapel Hill, NC 27516-6113
info@tortillacocina.com
This site carries presses and makers for both corn and flour tortillas, *comals*, griddles, lime squeezers, and big glass jars.

INDEX

ABOUT THE AUTHOR

Scott Wilson grew up eating hard shell ground beef tacos with orange cheese and iceberg lettuce . . . until the taco trucks arrived in his hometown of Redwood City, California. He now lives on his homestead in Oregon with his wife, two children, and animals. When he's not thinking about tacos, he's writing, gardening, cooking, making beer, teaching classes on herbal brewing and food preservation, and spending time with his family.

ACKNOWLEDGMENTS

Thank you to my family and friends for indulging my tacomania over the years, to the taco fanatics on the Chowhound forum, to the professionals who contributed recipes to this book (Jose Alvarado, Eric Williams, Patricio Herrera, Ryan Magarian, Nikki R. Cohen), to the taquerías that provided direct inspiration and guidance, and the innumerable taqueros who ply their trade daily and spread the taco gospel across the planet. And most importantly, a deep bow to the ancient farmers who made tacos possible by domesticating the venerable corn plant.